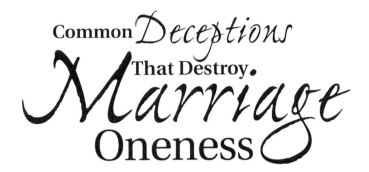

Common *Deceptions* That Destroy. *Marriage* Oneness

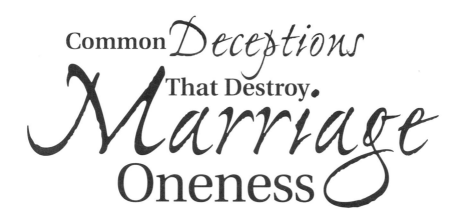

Common *Deceptions*
That Destroy.
Marriage
Oneness

Institute in Basic Life Principles
Oak Brook, Illinois

Common Deceptions That Destroy Marriage Oneness

Published by the Institute in Basic Life Principles, Inc.
Box One
Oak Brook, IL 60522-3001
Tel: 630-323-9800
Fax: 630-323-7271
www.iblp.org

The Institute in Basic Life Principles is a Biblically based, not-for-profit, nonsectarian training and service organization dedicated to serving families, youth, and leaders worldwide, through training in Biblical principles that bring true success in life.

International Standard Book Number: 0-916888-25-8 (paperback)

Cover design and interior layout: Kristen Hoopes
Photography: William Thornton (Front cover inset: Comstock Images)

Printed in the United States of America
Second Edition   020255   5/02
01 02 03 04 05 06 — 10 9 8 7 6 5 4 3 2 1

Table of Contents

The Destruction From Deceptions

The collapse of marriages in our day is a disaster that reaches far beyond the hurts and wounds of the couples involved. It devastates their children and establishes iniquities that are passed on for generations to come. Even marriages that appeared strong are now breaking up with new assaults, such as rampant pornography and intimate discussion with strangers in Internet chat rooms. However, a failed marriage can usually be traced to deceptions that have been believed and defended by one or both parties.

A year ago, I became aware of the marvelous results that Mike and Connie Walsh were experiencing with couples who had "hopeless" marriages. I asked them how they were able to get such positive and lasting victories. It is then that they explained to me the deceptions they were uncovering and removing in the lives of those whom they were counseling.

This book further expands and clarifies the seven deceptions that Mike and Connie explained at the Knoxville and Sacramento ATI Training Conferences in 2001. We trust that this book will be carefully studied so that marriages will achieve the potential God intended.

We realize that each marriage is different and that therefore this information must be wisely and prayerfully discussed and applied. We urge you to fully follow Biblical steps of action for removing each deception. May God give you the wisdom and grace to strengthen your marriage and raise up the foundations of many Godly generations.

 We had no idea when we were going through the storms in our marriage that we would learn valuable lessons that could help others in their marriages. We were equally amazed to discover that the things we were struggling through were being experienced by so many other couples.

We want to assure you that we come to you as fellow learners and that we are constantly open to new lessons and insights God teaches us so that we can pass them on to others. Our goal for our own marriage and for the marriages of others is to see God build a oneness of spirit in our lives and to raise up Godly children who can make an impact in our day.

We encourage you to consider using this book as a way to help identify hindrances that may be keeping your marriage from being all that God intends it to be. The evaluations at the end of each chapter are designed to reveal these hindrances. The evaluations may also be beneficial for couples considering marriage, to help uncover potential areas of conflict, by applying them to your relationships with your parents and other authority figures in your life.

A deception, by its very nature, has within it a grain of truth that allures us to believe it. Prayerfully consider each deception and whether its corrupt fruit of fear, bitterness, pride, and self-indulgence is being manifested in your marriage.

Mike and Connie Walsh

Chapter One

Deception Number One :

"Because of the 'curse' on Adam and Eve, wives desire to rule over their husbands."

Why is this a deception?

This statement is a deception because it clouds the fact that both the husband and the wife desire to control the marriage. God designed marriage to be under His control. As a result of the "curse," the husband views his wife as a competitor who desires to control the marriage, and responds to her accordingly.

The common misinterpretation of the "curse" in Genesis 3:16 is the idea that a wife will desire to compete with her husband for leadership. Genesis 3:16 says, "Unto the woman he said, I will greatly multiply thy sorrow and thy conception; in sorrow thou shalt bring forth children; and thy **desire** shall be to thy husband, and he shall **rule** over thee."

To overcome the "curse," the husband must patiently and lovingly listen to his wife and then get final direction from God.

The first consequence to Eve's sin was that she would experience pain in childbirth, and the second judgment was that she would desire her husband and that he would rule over her.

The word *desire* in Genesis 3:16 is the Hebrew word *teshuwqah*, which means "a stretching out after, a longing." It is derived from the word *shuwq*, which means "to run after or over, i.e. to overflow like water."

The Song of Solomon is a poetic discourse between a husband and his wife that is full of language and metaphors depicting love and its emotions of protection, desire, and care. This God-inspired book depicts the strength of love, the commitment of love, and the sweetness of love. It is an emotional picture of love as God designed it, with the hindrances to love removed. It is also a "picture" of the tender love of the Lord between Himself and His bride—the Church.

This book is intended to give hope to all marriages as we submit one to another in the fear of God. In the Song of Solomon, this word *desire* is used in a positive way: "I am my beloved's and his desire is toward me" (Song of Solomon 7:10). In this statement the woman is rejoicing in the joy and purity of having the storehouse of her husband's affections toward her. She would not be rejoicing if she had lost the "contest" of power with her husband. The passage could more accurately be read, "My beloved is mine and his heart's desire is toward me."

In the Song of Solomon, the word *desire* is used to describe the longing the husband has for a relationship with his wife.

Genesis 4:7 is the only other verse in which this word *desire* is used. God is warning Cain of pending disaster. "Sin lieth at the door. And unto thee shall be his desire, and thou shalt rule over him." Sin is personified as pursuing Cain, stretching itself out after him, and longing for a relationship with him while desiring Cain to find pleasure with it. But God admonishes Cain to "rule" over it. This is the picture of how we should treat sin. We should deal firmly with it. We should exercise dominion and power over it. Sadly, many husbands tend to treat their wives as they should treat sin by closing off their hearts to them!

> *A wife longs for the strong and loving leadership of a husband who seeks God's wisdom, not his own ideas of right and wrong.*

Rule is the Hebrew word *mashal*, which means "to have dominion, govern, reign, bear rule, have power." This, too, is a natural tendency that will have negative results if it is not under the control of God's Spirit. If a husband fails to learn how to be a servant-example and to lead his family and wife through love, his rule will be insensitive and domineering, causing his wife to feel that she is of no value to him.

In reality, a woman longs for a relationship in which her husband attentively hears her heart. Before a couple is married, the prospective husband listens to his bride-to-be and values her opinions. With this attitude, he wins her heart, and this is the attention that she believes she will receive in the marriage. After marriage, if he overrules her opinions and feelings in an insensitive and unloving way, she will react to his pride. Her reaction only confirms his conclusion that she is resisting his leadership. No longer are they operating in one spirit but as two competitors in which the husband sees himself, rather than God, as the final authority.

God's judgment upon Adam, apart from death coming upon all men, was not that his wife would rule over him, but that he would have to work by the sweat of his brow. "And unto Adam he said, Because thou hast hearkened unto the voice of thy wife, and hast eaten of the tree, of which I commanded thee, saying, Thou shalt not eat of it: cursed is the ground for thy sake; in sorrow shalt thou eat of

The "curse" is that Adam and Eve received what Satan promised them—becoming like gods and deciding for themselves what is right and what is wrong.

it all the days of thy life; Thorns also and thistles shall it bring forth to thee; and thou shalt eat the herb of the field; In the sweat of thy face shalt thou eat bread, till thou return unto the ground; for out of it wast thou taken: for dust thou art, and unto dust shalt thou return" (Genesis 3:17–19). Adam's judgment is, in essence, work pressures that will put further strains on the marriage relationship.

Just as men have an inborn desire for those things that relate to the "dust of the ground," from which they were created (their life work), so women tend to center their lives around a relationship with a man, because they were created from Adam's rib. Therefore this "desire" is natural, and as with the man, when these desires are under the direction of the Holy Spirit, they will bring fulfillment and will glorify God.

To see the bigger picture, we must understand what Satan offered to Adam and Eve. He promised that if they would partake of the forbidden fruit, they would "be as gods, knowing good and evil" (Genesis 3:5).

Consequently, Adam and Eve got what Satan promised them— the tragedy of the knowledge of evil, which brought with it shame and condemnation. After the Fall, Adam and Eve had to endure constant conflict—conflict that resulted from knowing "good *and* evil." God said, "Behold, the man is become as one of us, to know good and evil" (Genesis 3:22). In this arena of conflict between two "warring gods," the husband rules over his wife by rejecting or discrediting her opinions so that she feels belittled and of no value. In an equally wrong response, she may react to him in bitterness and even rebellion.

> *Oneness is achieved only when the husband and wife go to the Lord together to seek His mind and directives for their lives and follow them.*

As a further consequence of this "knowledge," the husband fails to see the need to seek direction from God or value and consider the cautions of his wife. Thus, in a very real sense, he becomes a god to himself and forfeits potential blessings that could be his through his God-ordained advisor and friend.

The Fall of Adam and Eve resulted in a tendency in every person to be his or her own boss. When pride is identified in either the husband or the wife, a major barrier that separates them is removed. A wife will be able to respond to her husband, and a husband will be able to receive his wife. According to God's design, one of the greatest desires of a woman's heart is to have the protection and leadership of a wise and loving husband. When a husband fails to exercise this kind of leadership in his marriage and family, his wife will be motivated to take matters into her own hands, causing her husband to react.

If a married couple is driving on a busy highway with their children in the back seat and the husband falls asleep at the wheel, the wife will instinctively reach over and grab the steering wheel to avert a disaster. It would be unreasonable for the husband to wake up and rebuke his wife for trying to "take over." The unfortunate fact is that many husbands have "fallen asleep at the wheel" and do not even know it. Wives attempt to get their husband's attention and warn of perceived dangers. Pride blinds a husband from his need for his wife, and as a consequence he is unable to take advantage of a "second set of eyes." He often does not see danger until there is an accident or disaster, and so in pride he rules over his wife.

What are the consequences of this deception?

When a man believes the deception that because of the "curse," his wife is trying to rule over him, he will see her as a competitor, adversary, or an enemy. In this hostile atmosphere, any concerns that the wife brings to her husband are viewed as an "attack." His perception will be strengthened if the wife expresses her concerns with strong emotions or has a spirit of pride herself.

Under these circumstances, a husband whose plan of action is questioned by his wife will react to his wife as being negative and faultfinding. This wrong response grieves and confuses her; she may wonder, "Why did he ask my opinion in the first place, since he does not listen to my concern anyway?"

A husband does not have to agree with everything his wife tells him. However, he should listen to her with an understanding heart. He must also discern what God is saying through her cautions. Many times, God will reveal insights to the wife that are needed by the husband in order to make wise decisions. Listening to and considering another's opinion or perspective is foundational to any close relationship.

The husband may not realize that his reaction to his wife could be based on his own insecurity of trying to be his own boss. Instead of thinking he can run his own life, a man must get clear direction from the Lord. He is to find God's will through Scripture, which he is to teach his wife and family. In this way he "cleanses" the wife by the Word as stated in Ephesians 5:25–26, "Husbands, love your wives, even as Christ also loved the church, and gave himself for it; That he might sanctify and cleanse it with the washing of water by the word." In this

> *A wife longs for a deep relationship with her husband, in which she may confidently submit to his Godly leadership.*

way, the very things that bother him about his wife become lessons of patience and opportunities to show acceptance and love as he leaves those things with God and allows Him to "wash" them away in His time.

What attitude is at the heart of the Fall? It is the attitude of pride. It was pride that caused Satan to be cast out of heaven, and pride that resulted in Adam and Eve's being cast out of the Garden. It is pride that causes contention between husbands and wives. Pride does not want to listen. It demands its own way. Solomon said it well, "Only by pride cometh contention: but with the well advised is wisdom" (Proverbs 13:10). A husband and wife are well-advised by listening to each other and also listening to the Lord through God's Word and prayer.

Any defensiveness in attitude or unwillingness to listen to counsel confirms pride. To conquer pride, the husband must acknowledge his need for God's wisdom and lead the family in crying out for it. God promises "If thou criest after knowledge, and liftest up thy voice for understanding; If thou seekest her as silver, and searchest for her as for hid treasures; Then shalt thou understand the fear of the LORD, and find the knowledge of God" (Proverbs 2:3–5).

If a husband sees himself as already having the final answer, he will obviously not recognize any need to check with God or to pray with his wife. Prideful men are reluctant to look to God for His mind on decisions, especially in the presence of their wives. This only complicates the problem of the husband acting as his own boss. He views conflicts as a choice of either his way or her way, rather than God's way.

When a husband and wife understand the judgments that God pronounced on Adam and Eve, they will see that they can be greatly alleviated, if not overcome. Adam and Eve sinned because they rejected God's program of headship as clearly defined in I Corinthians 11. "The head of every man is Christ; and the head of the woman is the man; and the head of Christ is God" (I Corinthians 11:3). One purpose of God's pronouncement on Adam and Eve was to restore the order of dependency that He had first established for them. Adam was to be dependent upon God, hence God cursed the ground, and the man now has to perform greater labor and painful toil to make a living. Ideally, this will motivate him to trust in God and receive the valuable benefit of his wife's counsel. Likewise, God's pronouncement upon Eve was intended to restore her dependence upon her husband and the Lord.

Why is this deception hard to overcome?

Pride judges others of its own wrong attitudes. Because of the blinding effects of pride and the "walls" it creates in any relationship, people will accuse others of the same wrong attitudes they have.

A prideful husband is tempted to elevate himself above his wife and children and to "lord over" them, misusing his position as head of the family. He demands obedience to his rules, whether they are wise or unwise, just or unjust. A prideful man feels like less of a man if he listens to a woman's opinion, or to anyone else's for that matter. He does not see her as:

> *An offended wife will use her bitterness to control her husband with the guilt of his past failures and pressure him to change.*

- Bone of his bone
- A necessary part of him that he cannot effectively live without
- A complement
- An essential helpmeet
- An indispensable resource
- A valuable companion and friend

This prideful husband may wonder why he is frustrated in his marriage relationship and why his wife does not trust in his leadership. In response to his pride, she may not only lack trust in him but actually resist him or reject his leadership altogether. If he is prideful, even God will resist him. (See I Peter 5:5.) A wise man will recognize his wife's lack of trust in his leadership and lack of respect for him as possible reproofs for pride.

A woman's pride often manifests itself by her unwillingness to accept her husband unless certain conditions are met, or by insisting on her own way. On the other hand, a wise wife will recognize the weakness of her husband but will accept his decisions as something that God will ultimately work through, for her good. In the case of her husband asking her to do that which is legally or morally wrong, she must appeal to him, explaining that both of them are under the higher Law of God and that she cannot participate in that which is contrary to His Law. (See Chapters 5 and 6.)

How does Scripture illustrate God's design for the marriage relationship?

In I Peter 3:7, God gives clear direction on how husbands and wives are to live together in harmony:

- "Husbands, dwell with your wives according to knowledge"— This includes listening to a wife's perspective, hearing her heart, and understanding how she perceives a situation.

- "Giving honor unto her as unto the weaker vessel"—This could also be said, "as unto the more delicate vessel," ("contents" are the same, but the "container" is weaker). A wife tends to be more sensitive to and is affected more by the words and attitudes of her husband than he is by hers. Husbands have a responsibility to exercise the greater strength of their vessel by restraining their wrong attitudes, harsh words, and careless statements. A husband who lacks wisdom has a tendency to belittle his wife, making her feel foolish, stupid, or even "crazy." He looks down upon her and makes light of her concerns. He fails to recognize her value.

- "As being heirs together of the grace of life"—A husband and wife are participants and fellow runners in the same race, recipients of the same prize, partakers of the same gift, joint heirs, and mutual receivers of the riches of God's abundant grace. They are to live arm in arm, hand in hand, side by side—together! They have the high privilege and calling of bringing children into the world and training them to be wise and Godly sons and daughters.

- "That your prayers be not hindered."—If the instruction of this Scripture is not followed, the husband will not experience the energy of being "connected" to God's "power supply." If prayers are hindered, the husband loses the power of effective prayer in dealing with the challenges of raising up a "Godly seed," walking in victory over sin's delusive power, and making wise decisions that will stand the test of time.

The "Alone" Test

"And the LORD God said, It is not good that the man should be alone; I will make him an help meet for him" (Genesis 2:18).

To be alone is to be:

- Separated
- Excluded
- Single-handed
- Ruled out
- Unaided
- Left out
- Without help
- Solitary
- Apart
- Isolated
- On your own
- Secluded

How do husbands go about their daily lives "alone"?

A man may think that because he is married and has a wife, he is not "alone." To help evaluate how "alone" you really are, take the "Alone" Test, giving your wife the freedom to express her honest feelings by grading you on a scale from 1 to 10.

_____ Does your husband include you in his planning and goals?

_____ Does your husband include you in a day-to-day understanding of what takes place at his work?

_____ Does your husband ask for your counsel before making decisions?

_____ Does your husband share his conversations with you?

_____ Does your husband include you in his relationship with God?

_____ Does your husband share his thoughts with you?

_____ Does your husband confide in you by sharing his dreams and desires with you? *(A score of 70 is a passing grade.)*

The "Help" Test

And the Lord said, "I will make him an help meet [help fitting] for him" (Genesis 2:18).

Help means:

- Uphold
- Stand by
- Cooperate
- Assist
- Aid
- Support
- Encourage

To see how much of a "help" you are to your husband, please allow your husband to share his honest feelings by grading you on a scale of 1 to 10.

How much of a "help" are you to your husband?

_____ Does your wife help you keep right priorities?

_____ Does your wife pray for you?

_____ Does your wife aid you in work?

_____ Does your wife support your decisions?

_____ Does your wife assist you in your plans?

_____ Do you sense that your wife admires and respects you?

_____ Does your wife encourage you when you are down?

_____ Do you sense that your wife wants to please you and do good?

(A score of 80 is a passing grade.)

One of the greatest battles a wife may have to face is the battle of humbling herself. If a wife is not submitted to her husband with reverence as unto the Lord, she needs to take responsibility for her response to him. (See Chapter 2.) A wife may react to her husband's bad decisions or hurtful actions. Yet, her response is just as important before God as her husband's actions are, and He will hold her responsible for it.

A wife can fall prey to our enemy's subtle temptations to react to her husband who is wrong. She thinks, "I am right!" She may be, but the attitude of "I am right" is the cause of many stagnant marriages. Scripture says, "It is better to dwell in a corner of the housetop, than with a brawling woman in a wide house" (Proverbs 21:9). Brawling denotes a contentious and competitive spirit. The root of a brawling attitude is pride. A wife is not to be the Holy Spirit or the conscience of her husband. She must have a track record of doing good for and being loyal to her husband so that her husband's heart may trust in her.

Only as a couple takes an issue to God in prayer, with an attitude of only wanting God's will, will there be a oneness of spirit.

A woman must discern when to let an issue go and when to make an appeal. In temporal issues, she must give her husband room to fail. In moral issues, she must make an urgent appeal. When there has been faithfulness in the past, her husband will be able to receive these appeals because he knows she is loyal. Loyalty is the only platform for an effective appeal.

There may come a time when a wife will not be able to go along with her husband. Then, he must know that it is not just a reaction on her part, but a sincere inability to endorse his actions.

A wife's humility will cause her to consider her own shortcomings. (See Galatians 6:1.) She will be patient with others because she understands that any change is the work of God (see I Corinthians 13), and she will not be frustrated or irritated with another's slow progress.

(See Matthew 18.) She will show mercy and patience because she realizes she has been forgiven much. (See Luke 7:47.)

What practical truths overcome this deception?

- Pursue her. (No matter what pressures you are under, she must sense that she is your first priority.)
- Relate to her. (See things from her perspective.)
- Pray with her. (She will be comforted to know that you understand what she is experiencing.)
- Don't "rule her out" or react, no matter what her attitude is!
- Take responsibility for your 10 percent. (Allow the Spirit of God to convict you, and humbly ask for forgiveness.)
- Don't go to bed angry. (Resolve the problem, no matter how late—God gives energy and grace to do His will.)
- Listen to her. (You don't have to fix it. One of the greatest hindrances to listening to a wife's concerns is being overwhelmed with other pressures. It is a freeing thought to realize that "fixing it" does not bring a wife as much comfort as does showing genuine concern by praying about the need with her and looking to God for the answer. This also does much to establish your leadership as your wife and family witness God's supernatural answers to those needs.)

If a husband does these things, by his sincere actions he will invite his wife to open her heart to him, and he will conquer pride. The way for a husband to overcome the deception is to see his wife's needs and reactions as opportunities to show Christ's love and compassion to her.

How the "Curse" Is Turned Into Blessing

As a result of the judgments that were put upon Adam and Eve, there will be "trouble in the flesh" in the marriage relationship. (See I Corinthians 7:28.) However, there are conditions that, if met, will minimize the consequences of the judgments that are upon them. The wife will be saved (receive much respect and honor) in childbearing "if she continues in faith and charity and holiness with sobriety"

(I Timothy 2:15). As the husband conquers pride, he will be able to accept the "help" that God designed his wife to be to him and receive the many benefits and rewards for doing so.

Oneness takes place when two people, with two totally different perspectives and opinions, submit their thoughts, wills, and emotions to the Lordship of Christ. In order to accomplish this, the husband and wife must both come to God, seeking His will in prayer. Neither one can maintain the attitude of "I'm the only one who is right." If there is a difference in opinion and a couple is deadlocked, an arbitrator should be called in.

An arbitrator is a mediator, referee, or umpire who rules on close plays. Who can be called for such an important position? We need someone who is discerning, who will not take sides, who will be available on a moment's notice, and who can be trusted as a confidant. God has provided such an arbitrator for all of His people—the Holy Spirit.

We must allow His peace to arbitrate: "Let the peace of God rule in your heart, to which also you are called in one body" (Colossians 3:15). The Greek word for *rule* means "to arbitrate." It is from the Greek word *brabeus,* meaning "umpire." It can be properly defined as "to umpire" or "call the play."

Only as a couple takes an issue to God together in prayer, with an attitude of not getting their wills but God's will, can they allow the Spirit of God to arbitrate through His peace.

Both the husband and wife will offer different perspectives to every situation. As each opinion is respected, they will be able to exhort one another as they seek God's ways. Their prayers will not be hindered. God will answer them and bring His power to the situation. Both will receive the benefits that God desires for them.

The Benefits of Overcoming the Deception
- Maintaining the excitement and newness of the marriage relationship—"Rejoice with the wife of thy youth" (Proverbs 5:18).
- Experiencing the rich harmony of "oneness" in your marriage—"Live joyfully with the wife whom thou lovest all your days" (Ecclesiastes 9:9).
- The joy of having a husband who overflows with the "desire" to love, provide for, and protect his wife—"I am my beloved's, and his desire is toward me" (Song of Solomon 7:10).

Confirming Testimonies

How a Hopeless Thirty-Year Marriage Was Transformed Into a Rich Relationship

Dear Mike and Connie, thank you for sharing! Your example and transparency before us was paramount. Nothing I have ever read or heard from the pulpit or in marriage seminars has had the life-changing impact that this idea of "oneness" has had. The ongoing blessing of knowing that my husband is listening and caring about all I say, think, and feel is wonderful. I am truly blossoming under this kind of love. I never thought marriage could ever be like what we are experiencing. I scoffed at people who appeared to be "syrupy" about their love for one another. I got to the point where I wanted no part of marriage, especially to my husband.

God has changed everything. The concept of His design for us being "one flesh" is so right. If I hurt, he does. If I'm concerned, he wants to understand why. I now care about his feelings, needs, and desires. We have a new "two-month-old" marriage and it's like a honeymoon. We have asked the Lord for forgiveness for thirty years wasted. We constantly thank Him for His mercy toward us.

—A transformed wife

How a Strong Man Became Mighty by Surrendering His Will

My wife and I have been married for almost thirty-five years. We love each other and have always enjoyed being together. In recent years, however, an old problem became a serious threat to our marriage. Whenever decisions needed to be made, especially important ones, we found ourselves dealing with increasing levels of conflict. These times of conflict became more frequent and were triggered by even the smallest issues. Our conflicts lasted longer and obviously began to affect the rest of the family. The children would either take sides or become very upset and emotional over each situation.

My problem was insisting on being in charge: "I, alone, make the decisions." My impression of my wife was that she did not like my decisions or that she always had a better idea. I thought she would find out what I thought and then pick the contrary position, or at least require significant changes to my ideas before she would agree or be supportive. Every aspect of our life together was affected, spiritually and emotionally, resulting sometimes in my taking off for several days to escape the stress and the conflicts. This did nothing to relieve the problems or instill confidence in my leadership with my wife and family.

We looked into counseling a number of times and sought advice from several respected Christian friends and pastors. Nothing squarely touched the root of the problem. The realization that she was bringing to me multiple, complex, seemingly impossible issues frightened me, and I was unable to do anything. Our situation worsened.

A short time ago, we heard how Mike and Connie had helped friends with their marriage, and we sought the Walshes help. After only about one hour of sharing with us, the Spirit of God opened my eyes to the truth that the "strong man" must be bound before his home can be plundered. I was a "strong man" but was preoccupied with how to "fix" the problems, resulting in feelings of inadequacy, which bound me and made me completely ineffective. This preoccupation kept me from doing the one thing that would break my bonds and lift my burden. I asked God to solve the impossible. I prayed, but it was "me-centered" and not God-centered. I needed to cry out for mercy, grace, and wisdom!

The Scripture and insights Mike and Connie shared set me free! For the first time in many years I understood how the marriage relationship was designed to work. The way I now see my wife's input changed from threats of my leadership, to the faithful warnings and suggestions of a trusted adviser and friend. Like salvation, this principle is so very simple. I had made it into something too complex, something I had to manage, not seeing that what I really needed to do was to hear my wife and turn to the only One Who could really "fix" the problem. Just as the centurion was a powerful man because he was a man under authority, the husband is powerful through Christ Who can do all things.

—A strengthened husband

Note: At the end of every chapter, there are evaluations for both the husband and wife. These should be the basis of praise, discussion and, if appropriate, clearing the conscience. These are intended to be filled out individually and then prayerfully discussed. Please consider concluding this time with the prayer given at the end of the evaluation.

Evaluation for the Husband

1. **Do you allow your wife to share her heart without criticizing or blaming her?**

   1 2 3 4 5 6 7 8 9 10
   Never   Always

2. **How would you rate your care and protection of your wife?**

   1 2 3 4 5 6 7 8 9 10
   Neglect   Excellent

3. **Do you take all problems to the Lord to gain His perspective rather than trying to fix them on your own?**

   1 2 3 4 5 6 7 8 9 10
   Never   Always

4. **Are you "married" to your work?**

   1 2 3 4 5 6 7 8 9 10
   Little   Much

5. **To what degree do you earn a hearing rather than demand one?**

   1 2 3 4 5 6 7 8 9 10
   Small   Great

6. **Do you react to you wife's suggestions or cautions?**

   1 2 3 4 5 6 7 8 9 10
   Always   Never

7. **Have you felt that your wife has used her bitterness against you to control your responses?**

   1 2 3 4 5 6 7 8 9 10
   Never   Always

8. **Do you believe God has given you authority that should not be questioned?**

   1 2 3 4 5 6 7 8 9 10
   Always   Never

O Lord, forgive me for believing that my wife is the cause of our problems. Forgive me for believing that she desires to compete with me. I am wrong for assuming the worst of my wife and for judging her. I acknowledge the damage that this deception has had on our marriage. I recognize that the "curse" is my pride that deceives me into thinking that I am able to make a decision apart from You and my wife's counsel. You desire a oneness of spirit in which we take everything to You in prayer. I do now give You back Your rightful place on the throne of my life and purpose that we will come to You in prayer as heirs together of the grace of life.

Date prayed: _____   Initials _____

Evaluation for the Wife

1. **Do you feel your husband allows you to share your heart with him without criticizing or blaming you?**

   1 2 3 4 5 6 7 8 9 10
   Never   Always

2. **How would you rate your desire to be a support and help to your husband?**

   1 2 3 4 5 6 7 8 9 10
   Weak   Strong

3. **Do you encourage your husband to take problems to the Lord instead of trying to fix them on his own?**

   1 2 3 4 5 6 7 8 9 10
   Never   Always

4. **Do you know when to let go of an issue?**

   1 2 3 4 5 6 7 8 9 10
   Never   Always

5. **Do you justify a negative attitude toward your husband because of the way he responds to you?**

   1 2 3 4 5 6 7 8 9 10
   Always   Never

6. **Is your husband open to your suggestions and cautions?**

   1 2 3 4 5 6 7 8 9 10
   Never   Always

7. **Have you used your husband's guilt over past failures as a "tool" to change him?**

   1 2 3 4 5 6 7 8 9 10
   Much   Never

8. **Do you believe your husband feels he has the right to unquestioned authority?**

   1 2 3 4 5 6 7 8 9 10
   Always   Never

O Lord, forgive me for believing that my husband is the cause of our problems. Forgive me for believing that he desires to compete with me. I am wrong for assuming the worst of my husband and for judging him. I acknowledge the damage that this deception has had on our marriage. I recognize that the "curse" is my pride that deceives me into thinking that I am able to make a decision apart from You and him. You desire a oneness of spirit in which we take everything to You in prayer. I do now give You back Your rightful place on the throne of my life and purpose that we will come to You in prayer as heirs together of the grace of life.

Date prayed: _____   Initials _____

Chapter Two

Deception Number Two:

"Little failures and inconsistencies should be overlooked because no one is perfect."

Why is this a deception?

This statement sounds reasonable. However, it violates the nature and character of God. On the one hand, God knows every detail of our lives, and "like as a father pitieth his children, so the LORD pitieth them that fear him. For he knoweth our frame; he remembereth that we are dust" (Psalm 103:13). On the other hand, He is a holy God and requires holiness of those who belong to Him. He states, "Be ye holy; for I am holy" (I Peter 1:16). God wants us to grow in maturity "till we all come in the unity of the faith, and of the knowledge of the Son of God, unto a perfect man, unto the measure of the stature of the fulness of Christ" (Ephesians 4:13).

By accepting the false notion that we can establish a standard of living that is lower than God's requirements, we put ourselves in His place, deciding what we can overlook and what others should tolerate. By so doing, we also place ourselves in opposition to what God wants to do in and through us. He wants to make us blameless and to present us faultless before the presence of His glory. (See Jude 24.) It is only by confessing and forsaking our faults and failures that the process of being made like Christ can continue.

The Consequences of Believing This Deception

Believing this deception results in major arguments in a marriage. They spring out of what one partner believes to be "insignificant" issues. Each partner will have faults and defects; however, as iron sharpens iron, so one partner should sharpen the other. By cutting off this person, the perfecting of character ceases and the potential of harmony in the marriage and achievements through teamwork in marriage are greatly diminished.

Statements That Communicate This Deception

- "I'm not perfect—what do you expect?"

- "You're exaggerating."

- "Your so 'nitpicky' about every little thing." (The very expression "nitpicking" refers to the process of removing lice from one's hair. Lice are little things, but one who has had them will testify about the great annoyance they bring. They make one feel "crazy" and as if his head is "crawling.")

- "Get over it! It's no big deal."

- "Why do you even bring it up? It's not worth mentioning."

- "Oh, I forgot." (This forgetful negligence communicates, "You are not a priority" or "This is not very important.")

- "I am struggling with that." (When the actual fact is that they feel there is no struggle at all, the truth is that there has not been any effort or attempt made to change. Those who say this minimize their problems and expect their spouses to overlook the inconsistency.)

- "That's just the way I am." (A spouse adds insult to injury when responding with this statement after the other gets up the courage to bring up a failure or inconsistency.)

These responses may minimize offenses in the mind of the one at fault. However, they magnify the fault in the other spouse's mind because now there is not only a flaw in behavior but also a defect in character. Excuses for our shortcomings will not be accepted by God. This type of thinking creates walls between a husband, wife, and the Lord. By expecting God and others to accept a certain level of failures and inconsistencies, we surrender areas of our lives to Satan's influence. He then uses these as a base of operation to build strongholds in our souls. Satan operates from these strongholds to defeat us, as well as those around us.

A further consequence of allowing "little" failures to exist in our lives is the damage they bring to the lives of our children. Children tend to copy the failures of fathers and mothers and justify these failures to an even larger degree. Thus, the iniquities of the fathers are visited upon their children to the third and fourth generations. "Visiting the iniquity of the fathers upon the children unto the third and fourth generation of them that hate me; and shewing mercy unto thousands of them that love me" (Exodus 20:5–6). Allowing little thoughts and failures in our own lives only evidences a lack of love. It is amazing how we can tolerate "little" failures in our own lives, but refuse to tolerate them in the lives of our children.

How does Scripture illustrate this point?

Scripture compares a little failure to such things as a little fire, a little leaven, a little fox, and a little seed. Each one of these begins small and grows larger, bringing with it various levels of destruction.

- A little fire—"Even so the tongue is a little member, and boasteth great things. Behold, how great a matter a little fire kindleth! And the tongue is a fire, a world of iniquity: so is the tongue among our members, that it defileth the whole body, and setteth on fire the course of nature; and it is set on fire of hell" (James 3:5–6).

- A little yeast—"Your glorying is not good. Know ye not that a little leaven leaveneth the whole lump? Purge out therefore the old leaven, that ye may be a new lump, as ye are unleavened" (I Corinthians 5:6–7).

Bacteria, viruses, and fungi are little "invaders." If allowed to grow, they may soon overtake the entire body with disease and destruction.

- A little fox—"The little foxes, that spoil the vines" (Song of Solomon 2:15).

- A little seed—"But while men slept, his enemy came and sowed tares among the wheat, and went his way. But when the blade was sprung up, and brought forth fruit, then appeared the tares also" (Matthew 13:25–26).

- A little more sleep—"Yet a little sleep, a little slumber, a little folding of the hands to sleep: So shall thy poverty come as one that travelleth, and thy want as an armed man" (Proverbs 6:10–11).

- A little folly—"Dead flies cause the ointment of the apothecary to send forth a stinking savour: so doth a little folly him that is in reputation for wisdom and honour" (Ecclesiastes 10:1).

The need to deal with our little faults and inconsistencies is very similar to the need of our immune system to deal with little bacteria, viruses, fungi, and other germs. If they are allowed to grow, they may eventually overtake the entire body with disease and destruction. Our challenge is to encourage the growth of good habits and restrain the growth of evil deeds.

Our natural inclination is to want to do evil and to enjoy the pleasures of sin. It is only by the power of God's grace that we can overcome the sinful tendencies of the lower nature.

Why is this deception hard to overcome?

We avoid dealing with little failures and inconsistencies because of our tendency toward slothfulness. Dealing with these issues is work! By our negative responses to those who point out our faults, we communicate that it is not worth the pain and effort to consider what they are saying to us. The principle of the "mote and the beam" helps illustrate what happens. (See Matthew 7:3–5.)

- The wife says, "You don't look at me when I'm talking."

If each takes care of his or her 10 percent, the rest will go away.

- He responds by making light of her comment with a rolling of his eyes and a deep sigh.

- The wife is hurt and begins to show irritation because he will not acknowledge that he indeed does do this.

- He finds fault with his wife for being irritated by such a "little thing." He views her irritability as 90 percent of the problem and his neglect to look at her as only 10 percent of the problem.

• She views her irritability as 10 percent of the problem and his lack of consideration for her as 90 percent of the problem.

The remarkable fact is that if they were both to take care of their 10 percent of the problem, the problem would be solved.

What practical truths overcome this deception?

By refusing to acknowledge our "little failures" and not asking forgiveness for them, we effectively short-circuit the very means of getting free from them. If we are not open to considering our failures and inconsistencies, no matter how little, we grieve the Holy Spirit Who convicts us. We also hinder His power, which we need in order to grow into a mature man or woman. "God resisteth the proud, but giveth grace unto the humble" (James 4:6).

Grace is the dynamic energy of God—it works in us to accomplish His will. (See II Corinthians 9:8.) It is the desire to do right and the power to do it. Without it, we will not have real and lasting changes in our lives. If we are to receive God's grace, we must be willing to humble ourselves, acknowledge our shortcomings (our 10 percent of the problem), and ask for forgiveness. The truth is that if we are not willing to humble ourselves in little matters, we will not likely humble ourselves in big areas either; pride will hinder our growth. If we fall prey to this damaging deception, we will greatly hinder the work of God in our lives.

We cannot question God's justice or reasonableness for requiring perfection of us when He knows that we cannot achieve it. His purpose is to give us a strong motivation to maintain continual fellowship with Him. He wants us to acknowledge our weakness and draw upon His strength for daily victory. When Paul discovered this truth, he exclaimed, "Most gladly therefore will I rather glory in my infirmities, that the power of Christ may rest upon me. Therefore I take pleasure in infirmities, in reproaches, in necessities, in persecutions, in distresses for Christ's sake: for when I am weak, then am I strong" (II Corinthians 12:9–10).

A spouse can be a "holy irritant," whom God uses to reveal the areas in our lives that we need to correct. When a couple gets married, they bring into the marriage the problems they were having when they were single. By virtue of the intimate nature of marriage, it is impossible to cover those failures for long. The right response to these shortcomings is not to ignore them, but to look them square in the face and come to the only One Who can change us.

The Power of Crying Out

God's way is to bring us into trials and troubles that are too big for us. When we realize that we cannot overcome them, He wants us to cry out to Him. Only when we cry out will He deliver us from our troubles. We are then to glorify Him with our praise and thanksgiving, which is what He desires. Thus He says, "Call upon me in the day of trouble: I will deliver thee, and thou shalt glorify me" (Psalm 50:15).

Many husbands and wives want to be held to a lower standard because they believe that the failures in their lives cannot be overcome. They have not discovered the power that God has for those who cry out for His deliverance. God gives the Holy Spirit to every believer to enable us to cry out to Him for the strength that only He can give for victory. "For as many as are led by the Spirit of God, they are the sons of God. For ye have not received the spirit of bondage again to fear; but ye have received the Spirit of adoption, whereby we cry, Abba, Father" (Romans 8:14–15). (See Romans 8:3–5.)

> *Many husbands and wives want to be held to a lower standard because they believe that the failures in their lives cannot be overcome.*

The power of crying out was demonstrated by the Lord when He told His disciples to take their boat across the Sea of Galilee. He knew this would be impossible because of a coming storm. Nevertheless, He got in the boat with them, and they began their trip. Soon the wind became strong and the waves crashed over the boat. The disciples had weathered many storms in the past and continued their journey until they finally realized that their very lives were in jeopardy. Only then did they cry out, "LORD, save us: or we perish" (Matthew 8:25), and only then did Jesus act to deliver them.

David was anointed by the Lord to be the king of Israel. Yet, for several years God allowed Saul to remain in that position and to bring David into many treacherous dangers. Through these, David learned the power of crying out on a regular basis. "Evening, and morning, and at noon, will I pray, and cry aloud: and he shall hear my voice" (Psalm 55:17). "When I cry unto thee, then shall mine enemies turn back: this I know; for God is for me" (Psalm 56:9).

Men are reluctant to ask for help, much less to cry out. Their pride and desire for self-reliance keep them from acknowledging their personal inadequacy and total dependence upon the Lord. However, by purposing to be faithful in little things as well as in big things, true character will be developed and demonstrated. "He that is faithful in that which is least is faithful also in much: and he that is unjust in the least is unjust also in much" (Luke 16:10). We must begin this faithfulness with each other.

When your spouse brings a little failure or inconsistency to your attention, it is important. It is worthy of serious consideration; it should be accepted as a challenge to overcome by crying out for the power of God and by setting up a program to conquer it.

Confirming Testimonies

How a Few Seconds of Selfishness Caused a Wife to "Foam at the Mouth"

We have a wonderful marriage and love each other very much, but the reality of the deception about little failures became very evident upon returning home after the ATI Training Conference. Had you not exposed this deception, I don't think we could have gotten through this one. This is what happened.

Both my wife and I were preparing to go to sleep. First of all, we have a very small bathroom. I was bent over the sink using the water. She was brushing her teeth. The time came for her to get rid of her mouthful of frothy toothpaste. She motioned to me that she needed the sink and could I move over. I was just about done, seconds away, so I gestured for her to wait. To my surprise, she seemed very irritated. She was literally foaming at the mouth!

Normally, I would have judged her, saying, "Why are you getting so irritated!" By considering her perspective, it became apparent that this was not the first time I had made her wait for me. I saw it. I saw how my little inconsideration of her was actually being selfish. Instead of reacting, as usual, I asked her to forgive me for what in the past seemed to me to be such a small thing. I was in the habit of just "blowing it off." I thanked her for revealing what should have been obvious! It is amazing how "little" things can create such big walls. —A more understanding husband

How Little Moments of Slothfulness Created a Mountain of Despair

When we got married, we had little Biblical background. I was following in the path of my father and grandfather. Both had a tendency towards sloth-fulness. Also attitudes of bitterness and resentment were passed down to my wife and were now an integral part of our marriage.

I had a very dominating father who intimidated me, and I married a Godly woman with lots of ideas and convictions. I always seemed to mini-mize her thoughts and didn't realize how hurtful this was to her. As a result of my slothful behavior, I did very little communicating with my wife. It became a way of life for us. I would listen only to pacify her, so we could move on. I didn't care as deeply as she did. I would commit to do some of the ideas she recommended only to end up not fulfilling a promise that I had made to her.

One of the commitments that I made was to discipline the children when they were disobedient. I ended up seldom disciplining them, which resulted in my putting tremendous pressure on the marriage. I knew I wasn't following through on different responsibilities, but they did not seem to be major issues. I could not see that the cumulative effect of my slothfulness was taking a major toll upon my relationship with my wife and children.

I did not realize how damaging the things I had excused as being inconse-quential or insignificant really were. Because I would look at it from only my perspective, I just could not see it. I had given up any hope of our relationship being restored. After thirty years of marriage and countless defeats, I found that when I received the truth that personal responsibility must be taken for "little" failures and that I should consider my wife's feelings ahead of my own, she responded to me! What I had given up on as impossible was restored in one day! —A delighted husband

Evaluation for the Husband

1. **Do you react to your wife about the "little" things she brings up to you?**

   1 2 3 4 5 6 7 8 9 10
   Always   Never

2. **Do you criticize your wife for making mountains out of what you believe are molehills?**

   1 2 3 4 5 6 7 8 9 10
   Always   Never

3. **Do you readily take responsibility for your "10 percent" of the problem?**

   1 2 3 4 5 6 7 8 9 10
   Never   Always

4. **Do you remind your wife that "nobody's perfect"?**

   1 2 3 4 5 6 7 8 9 10
   Always   Never

5. **When others point out your faults, do you tend to minimize them?**

   1 2 3 4 5 6 7 8 9 10
   Always   Never

6. **Do you compare your "little" failures with the "bigger" failures of others?**

   1 2 3 4 5 6 7 8 9 10
   Always   Never

7. **Do you react to "little" things that your mother or father tried to correct while you were growing up?**

   1 2 3 4 5 6 7 8 9 10
   Always   Never

8. **When shortcomings are pointed out, do you make an effort to change, instead of giving up?**

   1 2 3 4 5 6 7 8 9 10
   Always   Never

9. **When asking forgiveness, do you try to relive your offense through the feelings of your wife?**

   1 2 3 4 5 6 7 8 9 10
   Always   Never

O Lord, forgive me for believing this deception and thinking that these little failures of mine are insignificant. I now realize how hurtful they are to my wife and to You. I purpose by Your grace to take responsibility for every offense, no matter how small it appears to be.

Date prayed: _____ Initials _____

Evaluation for the Wife

1. **Do you react to the "little" things that your husband brings to your attention?**

   1　2　3　4　5　6　7　8　9　10
   Always　　　　　　　　　　Never

2. **Do you tend to disregard the little directives that your husband gives you each day?**

   1　2　3　4　5　6　7　8　9　10
   Always　　　　　　　　　　Never

3. **Do you readily take responsibility for your "10 percent" of the problem?**

   1　2　3　4　5　6　7　8　9　10
   Never　　　　　　　　　　Always

4. **When shortcomings are pointed out, do you make an effort to change, instead of giving up?**

   1　2　3　4　5　6　7　8　9　10
   Always　　　　　　　　　　Never

5. **When others point out your faults, do you tend to minimize them?**

   1　2　3　4　5　6　7　8　9　10
   Always　　　　　　　　　　Never

6. **Do you compare your "little" failures with the "bigger" failures of others?**

   1　2　3　4　5　6　7　8　9　10
   Always　　　　　　　　　　Never

7. **Do you react to "little" things that your mother or father tried to correct while you were growing up?**

   1　2　3　4　5　6　7　8　9　10
   Always　　　　　　　　　　Never

8. **Do your children react to little inconsistencies that you have justified?**

   1　2　3　4　5　6　7　8　9　10
   Always　　　　　　　　　　Never

9. **When asking forgiveness, do you try to relive your offense through the feelings of your husband?**

   1　2　3　4　5　6　7　8　9　10
   Always　　　　　　　　　　Never

O Lord, forgive me for believing this deception and thinking that these little failures of mine are insignificant. I now realize how hurtful they are to my husband and to You. I purpose by Your grace to take responsibility for every offense no matter how small it appears to be.

Date prayed: _____　　Initials _____

Deception Number Three :

"Most problems and hurts will go away if we just give them more time."

Why is this a deceptive statement?

This statement appeals to a man's tendency to procrastinate. It is false, because time does not heal difficult problems or untreated wounds. It only gives them greater opportunity to spread and infect other people.

Problems or hurts that are imaginary will usually go away with time because eventually it will be obvious that they were not real problems. However, even imaginary problems can produce real conflicts when they create wrong responses. A wife's hurt feelings over a husband's insensitivity or lack of leadership can become the real offense that creates walls in a marriage.

If real conflict can result from imaginary problems, how much more vital it must be to acknowledge the existence of and deal with actual problems! Every husband must realize that ignoring problems or failing to respond to them greatly hinders him from gaining

A wife tends to recognize problems and feel hurts more quickly and deeply than her husband.

the respect and confidence that he needs and wants from his wife and family. Every problem and hurt needs to be dealt with wisely and quickly, because time only deepens hurts and widens problems.

What are the consequences of this deception?

A wife tends to recognize problems and feel hurts more quickly and deeply than her husband. Meanwhile, a husband tends to ignore or refuse to acknowledge the symptoms of problems or hurts and deal with them only when they become major conflicts.

When a husband does not deal with matters quickly and wisely, his wife feels frustrated and unprotected. She loses confidence in her husband's leadership and either takes matters into her own hands or begins looking for help outside the marriage.

If the husband minimizes or discredits the concerns that his wife has, he is saying to her, "I don't value your perspective" or "Your opinion is not worth listening to." This type of prideful response communicates a rejection that is very painful for any person to bear.

Why is this deception hard to overcome?

1. Husbands tend to react to emotions.

When a wife is highly emotional or agitated about a situation, her husband will tend to react to her emotions rather than respond to the problem. He will probably conclude, "If I can just get her settled down, we can solve the problem." Meanwhile, she is thinking, "If I can just get him to understand the problem, I'll settle down."

In this situation, the husband must take the lead and focus on his responsibility to work on the problem rather than on his wife's emotional condition. Just by listening to the problem with concern and compassion, the husband will take a major step toward resolving the wife's emotional state and viewing the problem objectively.

He thinks . . .
"If I can just get her settled down, we can solve the problem."

She thinks . . .
"If I can just get him to understand the problem, I'll settle down."

2. Husbands may not know the solution.

A second reason that a husband does not tend to respond to a problem immediately is that he often does not know how to solve it. Instead, he feels overwhelmed and helpless and hopes that with time the problem will go away.

What most husbands do not realize is that they do not have to solve the problem. The wife just wants him to listen to her concerns, look into the matter, and bring the problem before the Lord in prayer.

3. Husbands often lack a "warfare mind-set."

If a husband does not realize the fact that he and his family are in a life-and-death combat with a relentless and treacherous adversary, he will assume that things "just happen" and that they are of no real consequence.

The fact is that Satan's goal is to steal, kill, and destroy; he will use every opportunity to accomplish his goals. (See John 10:10.) Thus, we are commanded to be good soldiers and to "war a good warfare." (See II Timothy 2:3 and I Timothy 1:18.)

Warfare requires vigilance and serious-mindedness at all times. We must always be aware that our "adversary the devil, as a roaring lion, walketh about, seeking whom he may devour" (I Peter 5:8). If a husband is to provide proper protection for his wife and family, he must recognize the tactics of this adversary.

Discouragement is one of Satan's most effective weapons against couples.

- **The tactic of discouragement:** One of Satan's chief weapons is to bring about discouragement. This is the immediate result when a husband fails to respond to the concerns that his wife brings to him. It does not matter whether these concerns are real or imagined, because the results are the same. Discouragement is one of Satan's most effective weapons against couples. At the base of every discouragement is a lie from Satan.

- **The tactic of fear:** Another major cause of defeat in a marriage occurs when the wife is "devoured" by fears. Fear, unbelief, and self-pity are all based on Satan's lies. A woman tends to be even more vulnerable to fears than her husband is. These fears activate her hormonal system and produce damaging physical consequences, such as anxiety attacks, asthma, allergies, sleep loss, and a host of other health problems. Therefore, even if the concerns of the wife are unfounded, her worry can produce health problems and attitude problems that are even more destructive than the original situation that caused them.

- **The tactic of bitterness:** None of us sets out to be bitter. It is a response to pain inflicted upon us. Bitterness is the result of not seeing suffering from God's perspective. Therefore, it is vital that we ask God for His wisdom and His purpose so that we can see how our suffering is not in vain. Bitterness focuses only on our pain, without considering the suffering the Lord endured to forgive us. (See I Peter 2:19–24; II Corinthians 1:4–7, 10.) God gives sufficient grace to every person to deal with problems and difficulties. However, we have the capacity to resist God's grace.

Somehow we convince ourselves that we have the right to be bitter or hold on to wounded feelings over the offenses of others. We do not realize that our bitterness and anger are motivated by our desire to have our spouses realize, at least somewhat, the hurts they have caused us. This is one of the major reasons we tend to hold on to our hurts. What we do not realize is that we simply are not designed to be able to hold on to a hurt without damaging ourselves and those around us. It is for this reason that God warns us to look "diligently lest any man fail of the grace of God; lest any root of bitterness springing up trouble you, and thereby many be defiled" (Hebrews 12:15). A bitter individual is like a drowning person—he pulls as many down with him as are within arm's reach. He "pulls down" those around him by sharing the details of his hurts. That "drowning" person is often full of fear and hurts and wants to protect himself.

> *Bitterness is the result of not seeing suffering from God's perspective, and a bitter person is like a drowning swimmer who pulls under with him anyone within reach.*

In a very real sense, many of the walls between husband and wife seem to be "mountains" that cannot be removed. It is only God's power that is able to remove them. Bitterness drives away the only real Source of Help we have, answered prayer. Jesus shared significant insights about these problems that are frequently overlooked.

"For verily I say unto you, That whosoever shall say unto this mountain, Be thou removed, and be thou cast into the sea; and shall not doubt in his heart, but shall believe that those things which he saith shall come to pass; he shall have whatsoever he saith. Therefore I say unto you, What things soever ye desire, when ye pray, believe that ye receive them, and ye shall have them. And when ye stand praying, forgive, if ye have aught against any: that your Father also which is in heaven may forgive you your trespasses" (Mark 11:23–25).

So, if you desire to claim the power that is available to you through prayer to have some "mountain" in your life removed, God will answer your need. The condition is that if you have "aught" against anyone, you must forgive as you would like to be forgiven, or God's power will not be released!

What truths can overcome this deception?

☐ **"Be swift to hear."**—James 1:19

Hearing each other's concerns does not involve simply listening to words. It requires a hearing heart, which is also able to detect a sense of urgency and a plea for full attention.

When Solomon was told by God to ask for anything he wanted, he requested an "understanding heart" in order to be a wise leader. (See I Kings 3:9.) The word for *understanding* in Hebrew means "to hear." Every husband needs a listening heart, especially when his wife brings to him a problem or a hurt. This process is key in establishing his leadership and resolving conflicts.

☐ **"Be slow to speak."** James 1:19

A vital key to overcoming anger in the marriage is for the couple to realize that their first and most important task is to simply listen to each other express their minds, wills, and emotions without reacting, defending, or trying to explain things. By patiently listening to each other's concerns and then graciously asking if there is anything else the other would like

The first and most important task in a marriage conflict is to simply listen to the partner without reaction or rejection.

to share, they are demonstrating love and respect for each other. The strong impulse to answer back or defend ourselves provides an opportunity to die to self and experience more of the power and life of Christ. Both should accept this opportunity from each other.

☐ **Respond in the day you hear of it.**—Numbers 30

God gives special authority to a father and a husband to annul an unwise vow that his daughter or his wife makes. However, that authority is only valid "in the day that he heareth" it. If he fails to respond to it on that day, the unwise vow stands, and any consequences that result from it are experienced. This example and others illustrate the importance of being alert to the need of dealing promptly with issues as they come up.

☐ **Search out the facts diligently.**—Proverbs 25:2

One who is in a position of responsibility not only must listen carefully to a matter, but must also diligently search it out. "It is the glory of God to conceal a thing: but the honour of kings is to search out a matter" (Proverbs 25:2). A diligent search is required of rulers, and diligent care is required of shepherds. Thus, Scripture exhorts, "Be thou diligent to know the state of thy flocks, and look well to thy herds" (Proverbs 27:23). Diligent inquiry means getting all the necessary facts and seeing the bigger picture so that the concern can be explained as either not as serious as was thought or serious and needing immediate attention.

> *When a husband ignores a conflict or hurt, he communicates a sense of rejection toward his wife and denial that there is a problem.*

☐ **"Agree with thine adversary quickly."**—Matthew 5:25

Jesus gives a clear mandate to not let conflicts continue but to deal with them before they escalate and cause damaging results. When a husband ignores a conflict or hurt, he communicates a sense of rejection toward his wife and even denial that there is any real problem. Such attitudes feed discouragement and bitterness and often cause the offended wife to take more drastic measures in order to get the attention of her husband. A husband must realize that he enlarges his circle of consequences when he does not deal with problems quickly. (See Matthew 5:26.)

☐ **"Let not the sun go down upon your wrath."**—Ephesians 4:26

Bitterness that is allowed to continue turns to wrath, and wrath breeds malice. The consequence of this sequence is that Satan is given a place of jurisdiction in the soul of the one who is bitter. Strongholds of false ideas are then built on the "ground" that has been surrendered. This results in destructive decisions and damaging emotions. Thus, we must give heed to the command: "Let not the sun go down upon your wrath: Neither give place to the devil" (Ephesians 4:26–27).

Steps to Forgiveness

☐ **Before asking forgiveness . . .**

- Is a change in my behavior necessary?
- Have I relived my offense through the feelings of my spouse?

☐ **In asking forgiveness . . .**

- Have I identified what offended my spouse the most?
- Does my wording imply that I blame my spouse or others?
- Am I trying to justify my offenses in any way?
- Am I trying to "preach" to my spouse?
- Is my confession an attempt to get my spouse to change?

☐ **After asking forgiveness . . .**

- How can I sincerely thank my spouse if he or she does forgive me?
- Am I prepared to respond correctly if my spouse does not forgive me?
- Could I ask my spouse to reveal further "blind spots" in my life?

How does Scripture illustrate this point?

No sooner had Solomon been appointed king of Israel than a bitter conflict was brought to him by two harlots. Each one claimed to be the rightful mother of a living baby and claimed that a baby who was suffocated the night before belonged to the other mother.

Because Solomon dealt with a conflict wisely and immediately, his kingdom was established under his leadership.

Solomon could have explained that he was too busy trying to establish his kingdom to deal with this "small" matter and that they should come back at a better time. Instead, he dealt with the conflict immediately and gave a wise and understanding decision. Word of his wisdom spread throughout the nation, and "all Israel heard of the judgment which the king had judged; and they feared the king" (I Kings 3:28).

Rather than being a distraction to his leadership responsibilities, the contention was the means of establishing his leadership in the hearts and minds of the people whom he served. Solomon had asked God for a wise and understanding heart, and God gave it to him. Every husband and father should ask God for such a heart and then use it for the conflicts that are encountered.

Because David failed to deal with the conflicts in his own family, it grew as a fire and soon engulfed Israel in a civil war.

We are given an opposite example in the life of King David. When his oldest son Amnon defiled his daughter Tamar (half-sister to Amnon), David failed to properly deal with the matter. Instead, he became angry and possibly hoped that time would resolve the problem and heal the hurts.

Because David failed to quickly deal with the matter, his son Absalom decided he would take matters into his own hands and kill his older brother for what he had done. (See II Samuel 13:1–32.) This incident, which started out as a domestic matter, smoldered in the heart of Absalom for two years and then exploded into a civil war. David's own immorality may have been at the root of keeping him from dealing with this conflict. This also illustrates one of the greatest hindrances to resolving conflicts—a guilty conscience. (See I Timothy 1:18–19.)

Confirming Testimonies

How a Husband Discovered the Key to Overcoming Anger

As a father, I was seriously dedicated to teaching our children morning and evening, as well as during teachable moments throughout the day, in the ways of God. We studied the Bible regularly, conducted daily character training, prayed together, and held each other accountable in character development. We did all the right things, but there was still something wrong.

I would say I was successful in every area, except in my marriage. My wife and I have been married for ten years. Before we married, I never felt I had a problem with anger, but after we married, I slowly discovered how serious a problem I had.

Every week we would get into an argument. Most of the time, I did not explode. I would close off my spirit to my wife. I would fume with hurt, twisted by a distorted perspective of what my wife was saying to me.

It took ten years to arrive at the conclusion that I was severely blind in some areas concerning our marriage relationship. The following were some of those areas.

- *I thought my wife did not understand me.*
- *I thought my wife did not respect me.*
- *I often perceived my wife as an enemy.*
- *I believed my wife was treating me like she was my mother.*
- *I did not think we needed counseling   for what I thought were a lot of good reasons.*
- *I did not think our marriage was in a critical state.*

Sometime in the spring of 2001, I took some advice from Mr. Gothard and cried out for God's deliverance from the things that angered me about my wife and our marriage. We went to Knoxville later that year. God had always brought about several major life-changing insights while at the conference.

This year there would be a major revelation also. When I listened to Mike Walsh, I saw myself. We had a similar past and faced similar marital problems. As I listened, I felt something happening on the inside of me. The Lord was doing a quiet yet powerful work in my heart. As I listened, I discovered several Biblical principles he was applying. I clearly saw the principle of the cross in everything he said. I saw him dying to pride and the desire to defend.

After listening to the testimonies, I knew I would be tested, and most probably at the conference. It happened after the morning session. Because of unconquered pride, I perceived any difference of my wife's opinion as criticism or attack. Pride prevented me from even considering her perspective. So that morning, when my wife mentioned a need that I should have taken care of but did not, I perceived it as her finding fault with me.

So often, when my wife makes a statement that is contrary to my own thinking, right away I put up my guard. She is surprised by this because she did not mean to be confrontational, but my pride assumes that she is. I felt she was criticizing me.

As I tried to listen to her perspective, everything inside of me wanted to react. An inner battle was raging. I began to see it—the source of my anger was rooted in pride. The truths I learned came to mind. I saw in my mind's eye the Lord laying down His life for me with all my pride and the resulting anger with its hurtful attitudes and words. I considered how the Lord, Who was without sin, "opened not His mouth" to His accusers. This was the hurdle I could not overcome in my marriage. Even God resists the proud, but He gives grace to the humble.

As soon as I humbled myself, it was as though the walls came down. I could see her perspective. I could respond to her without reacting. Pride was hindering our oneness. We now talk freely with each other and are able to bring our needs and concerns to the Lord.

—A humbled husband

How Seven Barriers Became a Bond to a Broken Marriage

After many years of marriage, we discovered that our early problems had only multiplied instead of dissipating. We had put up with each other's shortcomings while our children were growing up, but now with them gone, our communication had grown worse and worse. I still felt that there were areas that I could not conquer. My wife and I had gotten to the point of "psychological divorce." As we discussed our plight a few weeks before this seminar, we had very little hope; in fact, my wife said she had no hope! I felt terrible. We were both praying, but we had many walls that kept us from each other.

When we sat down to "talk things out" or "get to the bottom" of our troubles, we always came away worse or, at best, ended up in the same old stalemate. I was praying about seeking a Christian marriage counselor, though I really did not feel there could be someone who could truly show us God's viewpoint Biblically.

When the opportunity arose to go to Mike and Connie's marriage oneness seminar, we reluctantly agreed to attend. During the first two sessions, *the Lord really spoke to both of us, but especially to me. I had to learn so many things: like marriage is not a 50/50 proposition and that I need to be a leader **all** the time.*

*By the end of the third session and after several tearful and long conversations with my wife and with God, I discovered that it was not that I **could not** do the right things, but that I **would not** do them. I was making the wrong choices thinking that I could not be different. The Lord showed me that He was able, but that I had to want God and my marriage more than anything else. These are some of the things I thought I could not do:*

1. Be totally honest with my wife

2. Have daily devotions

3. Memorize Scripture

4. Pray with my wife daily

5. Lose weight

6. Control my eyes

7. Make the daily leadership decisions required as head of the house

God has shown me differently. My wife and I are now working on committing our sixth passage of Scripture to memory. I pray at least twice a day with my wife. I have lost nearly fifteen pounds. I have discovered that I truly can control my eyes. I am working on making the daily leadership decisions necessary for a true Christian husband to make.

Instead of "I can't," I discovered that "I refused." I said it was too hard, but praise God, I am discovering that "I can do all things through Christ Who strengthens me," and I "go in the strength of the Lord." We are going over the material page by page. It has been a time of strengthening the bond between us. We are finding that the only way we can work through this is by humbling ourselves, listening to the other's perspective, and then bringing all disagreements to the Lord together in prayer.

—Adapted from a committed husband

How Two Ugly Attitudes Eroded the Foundation of a Marriage

This deception hit me between the eyes. You see, we have been married for twenty-five years. When problems arose and we did not see eye to eye, instead of resolving it by seeking the Lord's guidance, we let it go. These unresolved conflicts were slowly eroding any goodness in our marriage. She began sleeping in another room. I allowed that to continue for years, content to live separate lives.

My pride kept me from understanding her hurts, and her bitterness kept her from forgiving me of these hurts. What a vicious cycle. How foolish we were to think problems and hurts would go away. Time only caused us to drift further apart until one day we barely knew each other.

Thank you for exposing these lies and giving us tools to be doers of the Word and not hearers only, deceiving ourselves.

—Excerpts from convicted husbands

Evaluation for the Husband

1. Do you have problems now that you thought would go away years ago?

1 2 3 4 5 6 7 8 9 10
Many   None

2. Do you ignore or belittle your wife when she keeps bringing up old problems?

1 2 3 4 5 6 7 8 9 10
Always   Never

3. Do problems that you have learned to live with irritate your sons and daughters?

1 2 3 4 5 6 7 8 9 10
Much   Little

4. Are there issues you have decided not to discuss because you cannot agree on a solution?

1 2 3 4 5 6 7 8 9 10
Many   None

5. Have you learned to live with problems that you promised your wife in the past you would take care of?

1 2 3 4 5 6 7 8 9 10
Always   Never

6. Do you wait for your wife to admit her faults before you admit yours?

1 2 3 4 5 6 7 8 9 10
Always   Never

7. Do you escape from problems by eating, sleeping, working, or walking out?

1 2 3 4 5 6 7 8 9 10
Always   Never

8. Have you suffered major consequences for problems that could have been resolved easily?

1 2 3 4 5 6 7 8 9 10
Many   None

O Lord, forgive me for believing this deception and allowing time to deepen problems and hurts. Forgive me for harboring bitter and prideful thoughts. I will now accept my personal responsibility, listen to the concerns of my wife, and then bring our problems to You in earnest prayer.

Date prayed: _____   Initials _____

Evaluation for the Wife

1. Do you have problems now that you thought would go away years ago?

1   2   3   4   5   6   7   8   9   10
Many   None

2. Do you ignore or belittle your husband when he keeps bringing up old problems?

1   2   3   4   5   6   7   8   9   10
Always   Never

3. Do problems that you have learned to live with irritate your sons and daughters?

1   2   3   4   5   6   7   8   9   10
Much   Little

4. Are there issues you have decided not to discuss because you cannot agree on a solution?

1   2   3   4   5   6   7   8   9   10
Many   None

5. Have you learned to live with problems that you promised your husband in the past you would take care of?

1   2   3   4   5   6   7   8   9   10
Always   Never

6. Do you wait for your husband to admit his faults before you admit yours?

1   2   3   4   5   6   7   8   9   10
Always   Never

7. Do you escape from problems by eating, sleeping, working, or walking out?

1   2   3   4   5   6   7   8   9   10
Always   Never

8. Have you suffered major consequences for problems that could have been resolved easily?

1   2   3   4   5   6   7   8   9   10
Many   None

O Lord, forgive me for believing this deception and allowing time to deepen problems and hurts. Forgive me for harboring bitter and prideful thoughts. I will now accept my personal responsibility, listen to the concerns of my husband, and then bring our problems to You in earnest prayer.

Date prayed: _____   Initials _____

Chapter Four

Deception Number Four :

"Marriage partners have a right to some privacy."

Why is this a deception?

In marriage, God makes two "one flesh." Any time a marriage partner conceals something, knowingly or unknowingly, it promotes a way of life that encourages them to lead separate lives. When this violation of God's design takes place, doubt, mistrust, and skepticism will surely creep in.

This pattern of secrecy begins subtly. You do not deliberately hide things from your spouse; you just think, "Why does my spouse need to know?" This thinking develops into a gradual process that is contrary to God's design for oneness in marriage. Oneness is built when there is complete openness in every area of each other's lives. This is not intended to rule out agreed-upon times alone with the Lord or discretion in modesty.

> *Secrecy requires darkness. However, fellowship requires light.*

Secrecy is based on darkness, and fellowship is built on light. Only as a couple walks in the light of openness and transparency will they enjoy true fellowship. This is the statement of Scripture, "But if we walk in the light, as He is in the light, we have fellowship one with another, and the blood of Jesus Christ his Son cleanseth us from all sin" (I John 1:7).

A further deception in this statement is that it violates the very nature of the marriage relationship. When two people enter into the covenant of marriage, they voluntarily and fully surrender to each other all their personal and private rights. For either party to retain the right of privacy is to damage the spirit of love and to violate the covenant.

A covenant is established on total trust. Requiring privacy is an open acknowledgement that one has something to hide, or that the other party is not trusted. Such mistrust in marriage can be formalized in a prenuptial agreement or just assumed or discussed before marriage. These agreements are based on distrust, and for this reason the terms of the agreement must be written and agreed to by both parties. Scripture does not refer to marriage as a contract but rather as a covenant. "The LORD hath been witness between thee and the wife of thy youth, against whom thou hast dealt treacherously: yet is she thy companion and the wife of thy covenant" (Malachi 2:14).

Secrecy is also a violation of God's design for man and woman. The husband is to protect his wife. If he does not know what is going on in her private activities, he will not have any understanding of how to protect her. Likewise, the wife is to be a help and a support to her husband. If she does not understand the details of his activities, she will not be able to be the help God designed her to be, especially in giving protective cautions to him.

What are the consequences of secrecy?

Secrecy in marriage creates walls of division. A demand for privacy is like one partner saying to the other, "I gave you my heart in marriage, but I want to keep you out of certain parts of it." Thus, it damages the very foundation of marriage and provides the basis for misunderstanding, suspicion, accusations, and argumentation.

> *Demanding privacy is like saying, "I gave you my whole heart, but I want to keep you out of parts of it."*

Marriages of more than twenty-five years are being destroyed because wives are involving themselves in chat rooms and fantasy, such as novels and television programs. They are privately attempting to have their emotional needs met apart from their husbands. If these wives would have told their husbands what they were secretly doing to have their needs met, it could have sounded the alarm for their husbands to do something to meet the need.

Husbands are leaving wives after becoming emotionally involved with a co-worker and/or pornography, all because they kept a part of their lives secret. Had the husband shared his conversations or activities with his wife, his wife would have immediately sensed danger.

Often this destruction results because a man spends long hours on the job without including his wife in the events of his day. He comes home tired. He rationalizes that his wife does not really need to know about his day and that the effort required to share really is not worth it.

> *A desire for secrecy is clear evidence of involvement in activities that will not pass the test of God's light.*

Soon this thinking becomes a habit. Without even realizing it, he is encouraging his wife to have her needs met elsewhere, and they drift further and further apart emotionally. This emotional disconnection results in an indifference and aloofness towards his wife. He is now "set up" for the "strange woman" to come along and meet his needs. He has forgotten God's warning: "Let not thine heart decline to her ways, go not astray in her paths. For she hath cast down many wounded: yea, many strong men have been slain by her. Her house is the way to hell, going down to the chambers of death" (Proverbs 7:25–27).

How does Scripture illustrate this point?

A person who demands privacy needs to discern whether his or her request is based on activities that would not pass the scrutiny of God's light: "Men loved darkness rather than light, because their deeds were evil. For every one that doeth evil hateth the light, neither cometh to the light, lest his deeds should be reproved. But he that doeth truth cometh to the light, that his deeds may be made manifest, that they are wrought in God" (John 3:19–21). Privacy provides the environment necessary for sin to grow. "When lust hath conceived, it bringeth forth sin: and sin, when it is finished, bringeth forth death" (James 1:15).

God further admonishes us that He "shall bring every work into judgment, with every secret thing, whether it be good, or whether it be evil" (Ecclesiastes 12:14). "For nothing is secret, that shall not be made manifest; neither any thing hid, that shall not be known and come abroad" (Luke 8:17).

We laugh when children cover their eyes with their hands and say, "You can't see me," but sadly, without even considering it, we often think the same about God. Because we do not see Him, we think He does not see us. We deceive ourselves into thinking that He is unaware of our actions, when in truth He is aware not only of our actions but He "understandest my thought afar off" (Psalm 139:2). He not only sees us in the light of day, but "the darkness hideth not from . . . [Him]; but the night shineth as the day: the darkness and the light are both alike to . . . [Him]" (Psalm 139:12). "Shall not God search this out? for he knoweth the secrets of the heart" (Psalm 44:21). We would be wise to consider the timeless truth, "Be sure your sin will find you out" (Numbers 32:23).

> *There is nothing in our lives that can be hidden from the Lord since the light and the darkness are alike to Him and He will bring every work into judgment.*

The heart that God will honor is that of David, who prayed, "Who can understand his errors? cleanse thou me from secret faults" (Psalm 19:12). It is significant that one of God's judgments for David's "secret" sins was that it would be proclaimed throughout the ages: "For thou didst it secretly: but I will do this thing [expose his sin] before all Israel" (II Samuel 12:12).

It is God's desire for all of us to uncover our sins so we can receive His mercy. "He that covereth his sins shall not prosper: but whoso confesseth and forsaketh them shall have mercy" (Proverbs 28:13). This is the sure promise of God. He is a God of mercy and a God to be feared.

Why is this deception hard to overcome?

We are under the false impression that our actions do not affect others, including spouse or children. Our thinking is, "What you do not know will not hurt you." The opposite is true. A spouse *will* receive the negative effects of the other's actions. This is the reality of oneness. Scripture is clear: "None of us liveth to himself, and no man dieth to himself" (Romans 14:7)—especially in marriage!

In our physical bodies, the head is the center for all decisions and direction. The entire body is affected by any and all choices the head makes. If the head makes a decision to endanger itself, does not the rest of the body have to pay a price? Of course! To think otherwise is irrational. We would laugh at any idea to the contrary. Similarly, "the husband is the head of the wife, even as Christ is the head of the church: and he is the saviour of the body" (Ephesians 5:23).

The decisions Christ made greatly affected us. He decided to suffer a cruel death on a cross, which brought incredible benefits to the rest of His "Body." Those who embrace Him as their "Head" will enjoy the benefits of the abundant life now and will relish in unspeakable splendor of an eternity of endless bliss.

By virtue of God's design for the husband-wife relationship, the wife is similarly affected by the decisions of her husband. He is the head of the wife. His actions and decisions will affect her.

Another reason this deception is hard to overcome is that we fall into the trap of living separate spiritual lives. When we have our private times alone with the Lord, which is right and good, but do not share from them with our spouse, what was meant to strengthen the relationship can cause division and reaction.

Those who demand this kind of privacy are not walking in the footsteps of the Lord, which they proclaim to be following. "Henceforth I call you not servants; for the servant knoweth not what his lord doeth: but I have called you friends; for all things

For a couple to be best friends, they must share the secrets of their hearts and their walks with the Lord.

that I have heard of my Father I have made known unto you" (John 15:15). This kind of relationship with the Lord, where the husband shares the insights and answers to prayer that the Lord gives him, cultivates a oneness not only with each other, but with the Lord. A wife who experiences this kind of sharing from her husband will not have any problem encouraging him to have private time with the Lord.

Christ showed His love for His disciples by spending time with them and sharing His thoughts and heart with them. He prayed, "That they all may be one; as thou, Father, art in me, and I in thee, that they also may be one in us: that the world may believe that thou hast sent me" (John 17:21).

It is wrong to think you can maintain a strong relationship with the Lord if there is a wedge in the relationship with your spouse. If things are not right with your spouse, serious efforts must be made to resolve them. "If we love one another, God dwelleth in us," but "if a man say, I love God, and hateth his brother [husband or wife], he is a liar: for he that loveth not his brother whom he hath seen, how can he love God whom he hath not seen?" (I John 4:12, 20). There is no way we can continue a close relationship with God when we maintain ill feelings toward a spouse.

What practical truths can help us overcome this deception?

Do not allow past failures to be kept private.

One of the most difficult areas of openness in a marriage is sharing past moral failures. There is Biblical wisdom for avoiding the explicit details of that which was done in secret: "Discretion shall preserve thee, understanding shall keep thee" (Proverbs 2:11). However, each marriage partner should know the specific types of failures that the other partner has had in the past, since keeping them secret provides an opportunity for Satan to bring guilt, fear, condemnation, and lack of spiritual growth.

Keeping failures secret provides an opportunity for Satan to bring guilt, fear, condemnation, and lack of spiritual growth.

"For ye were sometimes darkness, but now are ye light in the Lord: walk as children of light: (For the fruit of the Spirit is in all goodness and righteousness and truth;) Proving what is acceptable unto the Lord. And have no fellowship with the unfruitful works of darkness, but rather reprove them: For it is a shame even to speak of those things which are done of them in secret. But all things that are reproved are made manifest by the light: for whatsoever doth make manifest is light" (Ephesians 5:8–13).

Ideally, past failures should be shared prior to marriage, thus avoiding the damage of secrecy in marriage and the conflicts that result. Scripture shows that confession and prayer are vital keys to healing marital strife and gaining oneness. "Confess your faults one to another, and pray one for another, that ye may be healed. The effectual fervent prayer of a righteous man availeth much" (James 5:16). (See also Proverbs 28:13.)

Exposing past failures to the light is an important step necessary in bringing about true oneness.

Have a spirit of genuine repentance. Since a believer is "light" and instructed to walk in light, all that is done in secret must be brought to the light and reproved. When past failures are revealed, the other partner usually experiences deep hurt and grief. This is especially true if the offending spouse is merely stating the facts of what he or she has done. For heartfelt forgiveness to be given, the offending spouse should have a spirit of repentance by reliving the offense through the eyes of the other partner. It is painful when a spouse does not sense a spirit of genuine repentance.

Genuine repentance is seeking to restore the relationship with God and a spouse by taking responsibility for past attitudes and actions.

Genuine repentance is seeking to restore the relationship with God and a spouse by taking responsibility for the underlying attitudes of the offense. In contrast, the motivation of insincere repentance is only to receive the benefits of a restored relationship and not the restoration of the relationship itself.

Only if a husband and wife are completely committed to being honest and seeking proper forgiveness, can lost "ground" be recovered. Oneness with each other is then strengthened, and what Satan meant for evil, God amazingly works out for good. When a wife senses that her husband is committed to the Lord and to her, she is able to respond to him, and vice versa. With this commitment, they can begin working together for cleansing and continued victory.

Secret addictions of lust, pornography, drugs, and gambling are tremendously difficult to break. However, major victories are being experienced by those who have followed these principles. In this way the power of Satan can be broken and the power of light and love can become operative.

Confirming Testimonies

How the Pain of Openness Conquered the Power of Lust

I meant to write you this letter when I returned home from Knoxville. I am glad, however, that I got to share with you personally this afternoon what the Lord has done in my life. I have shared my moral failures with my wife and children and experienced the Lord's forgiveness and their forgiveness. However, I was still burdened by an unclean spirit of lust. My lust would cause me to fear that I would fail again and damage the spirit of my wife and our marriage. I was deceived into believing I could direct my lust toward my wife and that would be all right. My spirit would convict me that lust in any form was sin, but I could easily ignore it. I could not conquer this problem.

I had no control whatsoever over the flesh, and it showed up in other areas of my life. I gained weight because of my lust for food. I also have always had a spirit of anger. Though I have failed miserably, God has blessed my wife and me with a very transparent relationship. I realize now that because of my lust it was not as transparent as I thought. At the Knoxville Training Conference, God gave deliverance from the unclean spirit of lust. After the session on the seven deceptions in marriage I felt as though Mike Walsh had stood and told my story to the whole world. The same light that exposed his spirit of lust exposed mine also.

All I could do was to cry out to the Lord to deliver me. The Lord gave a wonderful confirmation of His deliverance the next morning when you met with all the fathers. You led us all to cry out to the Lord to deliver us. My wife is such a precious example of a Godly woman with a quiet and meek spirit. Our semitransparent relationship had revealed my lustful tendencies, and she knew there was a problem.

She had no idea how bad a problem I had with lust. I had been able to hide a very dark side of my life from her. I knew it would hurt her deeply when the light of truth exposed my sin.

I have never done anything to cause her to cry. When I shared with her this sin, she wept openly. It is a sad thing, and I wept over what I had done to hurt her. She forgave me, but I sensed I had damaged her trust in me. My fear of the Lord had been replaced by lust. I could not conquer this impossible situation.

Initially, my wife had reacted to the idea of a wife appealing to her husband when she sensed something was wrong. When my wife realized the destructiveness of this sin, she understood more clearly the responsibility of an appeal and the love that is demonstrated when a wife is willing to take the risk of doing so.

God is so good! In His mercy, He has restored the spirit of our marriage in answer to our crying out to Him. I have been set free! I now recognize my problem for what it is. The fear of the Lord has returned, and by His grace, we have overcome this deception! —*A triumphant couple*

How the Right Question Explained the Cause of Wrong Emotions

Thank you for addressing these major issues. My husband and I have a good marriage. Both of us are committed to the Lord and each other. Recently though, within the last year or so, I have been full of feelings of insecurity that were never there before: feelings of rejection, of feeling "fat" and "ugly," and it is not that I have gained weight or had any other physical changes. I could not figure it out. A strange distance seemed to be between my husband and me. Why was I feeling like this all of a sudden?

After hearing you share this deception, I thought I needed to ask my husband a question. "Is there anything you need to tell me that you are doing in secret?" I calmly asked, being nowhere near ready for how he was going to answer. He replied, "I have been waiting a long time for you to ask me." I was surprised. "You're kidding?" I said. He became very quiet, then looked at me soberly. Slowly he began, "Several months ago, I came upon an unusual web address. I was intrigued by it and out of curiosity, I went to that address. It was a pornographic site, and ever since, I have returned to it off and on."

I was shocked and saddened. He asked forgiveness, and I sensed that he was genuine and wanted out of this trap. I wondered if the negative feelings I had experienced came at the same time he had done these things. They completely coincided! I told him what was happening to me emotionally. We marveled at how what my husband had done had affected me, and I am sure it would be vice versa.

God's design of joining husband and wife together is a great mystery. We are one even when we don't acknowledge that oneness. We are working to reclaim our lost "ground" by asking the Lord to take back that "base of operation" we had surrendered to the enemy. This process of confession and forgiveness is painful as you well know, but I can testify that He is healing and cleansing just as He said He would. "If we confess our sins, He is faithful and just to forgive us of our sins, and to cleanse us from all unrighteousness" (I John 1:9).   —*Adapted from a relieved wife*

How a Twelve-Year Secret Blocked an "Ideal" Marriage From Oneness

I am writing to plead with you to get the message out that there is healing to be found after the devastation of lust and pornography. Your ministry has been good in encouraging men to avoid these things, but it seems that most men are not about to admit they actually have a problem in this area.

For some reason it is a very secret sort of sin. It usually goes unnoticed until it is too late. And then what? A man can lust in his mind, and no one can tell or see. This is why so many women are shocked when they find out. Whether the affair remains only within your husband's mind or becomes physical, it hurts all the same. The pain goes to the pit of a woman's stomach, making her feel like throwing up and of course absolutely helpless. We also feel as if it is "all our fault" and wonder what we have done to cause it.

Women need to know that in most cases the root cause goes much further back than before they were married and that they did not have anything to do with this sin in their husband's life. Granted, I do realize that we all have areas that we can change and grow in, but for the most part men have been exposed to pornography at an early age, and thus the seed is planted, and they struggle with the sin of lusting throughout their lives. The Lord can break this cycle of devastation and bring healing and oneness like never before in a marriage by getting to the root cause—as you often teach.

Please encourage men to be careful as they seek counseling, as the counseling my husband sought was not Biblical. He was told not to come to me and seek restoration, nor to tell me that he had this problem. My husband was told to find someone other than me to keep him accountable, but he never found anyone.

My husband finally got to the point that his conscience was eating him up, and he broke down and told me the whole story of how he was exposed as a child to pornography, and this carried over into his teen years. I was in shock to say the least. I had been married for twelve years and had no idea about his constant battle with lust. My husband has always been such a wonderful father and husband, so patient in all of our marital problems, and seemed to be striving for Godly standards and leading his children daily in God's Word. Everyone loves him. All my family and friends have always envied me because he is such a helper and loves his family. Then to find out that here I had lived with someone that had a whole separate life in his mind that I had no idea about? After my husband repented, I forgave him. (I praise God for your ministry, teaching me the fundamental s of forgiveness!)

I still had to deal with the hurt. I am still in the process of healing, but to see the freedom and new life in my husband makes it so worth the journey! He has truly become a man after God's heart, and the oneness that has occurred within our relationship is so amazing. I am continually humbled and overwhelmed at how good the Lord can be. I have struggled with the thought, "Something has got to be wrong with me, and that is why we have a lack of true oneness," but it was the stronghold that Satan had upon my husband, and this carried over into our home and marriage.

I am now my husband's number-one accountability partner. Even though it is embarrassing for men to talk about this whole subject, men need to be encouraged to be open before their wives. Their wives need them to be. This helps bring healing and trust back into the marriage. This also continues to bring them into a closer relationship with the Lord.

—A forgiving wife

Evaluation for the Husband

1. Has your thinking been, "Why does my wife need to know?"

1   2   3   4   5   6   7   8   9   10
Always   Never

2. Have you believed the lie that "What they do not know will not hurt them"?

1   2   3   4   5   6   7   8   9   10
Always   Never

3. Do you long for time away from your wife and conclude, "I need some space"?

1   2   3   4   5   6   7   8   9   10
Always   Never

4. Do you have difficulty being completely honest?

1   2   3   4   5   6   7   8   9   10
Always   Never

5. Do you tell your friends things you are afraid to tell your wife?

1   2   3   4   5   6   7   8   9   10
Many   None

6. Are there areas of your life that you refuse to let your wife be involved in?

1   2   3   4   5   6   7   8   9   10
Many   None

7. Is there anything you are doing in secret that you have not yet told your wife about?

1   2   3   4   5   6   7   8   9   10
Many   None

8. Are there things in your past that you have purposed not to tell your wife?

1   2   3   4   5   6   7   8   9   10
Many   None

O Lord, forgive me for believing the deception that I can withhold part of my life, no matter how small, from my wife and still expect a deep relationship with her. You have admonished us that if we walk in the light as You are in the light, we have fellowship with one another. I purpose to bring all things, past and present, to Your light so I can experience the joy of the fellowship You designed marriage to bring. Forgive me for believing that what I do in private will not affect my wife. I do purpose to be honest with my wife and ask for forgiveness for my failures out of a spirit of humility. I realize that the only sin You will not forgive is the one I refuse to confess.

Date prayed: _____   Initials _____

Evaluation for the Wife

1. Has your thinking been, "Why does my husband need to know?"

1	2	3	4	5	6	7	8	9	10
Always									Never

2. Have you believed the lie that "What they do not know will not hurt them"?

1	2	3	4	5	6	7	8	9	10
Always									Never

3. Do you long for time away from your husband, thinking, "I need some space"?

1	2	3	4	5	6	7	8	9	10
Always									Never

4. Do you have difficulty being completely honest?

1	2	3	4	5	6	7	8	9	10
Always									Never

5. Do your friends know things you are afraid to tell your husband?

1	2	3	4	5	6	7	8	9	10
Many									None

6. Are their areas of your husband's life that he refuses to let you be involved in?

1	2	3	4	5	6	7	8	9	10
Many									None

7. Is there anything you are doing in secret that you have not yet told your husband about?

1	2	3	4	5	6	7	8	9	10
Many									None

8. Are there things in your past that you have purposed not to tell your husband?

1	2	3	4	5	6	7	8	9	10
Many									None

O Lord, forgive me for believing the deception that I can withhold part of my life, no matter how small, from my husband and still expect a deep relationship with him. You have admonished us that if we walk in the light as You are in the light, we have fellowship with one another. I purpose to bring all things, past and present, to Your light so I can experience the joy of the fellowship You designed marriage to bring. Forgive me for believing that what I do in private will not affect my husband. I do purpose to be honest with my husband and ask for forgiveness for my failures out of a spirit of humility. I realize that the only sin You will not forgive is the one I refuse to confess.

Date prayed: _____   Initials _____

Chapter Five

Deception Number Five:

"A wife should focus on submission, whether her husband is right or wrong."

Why is this a deception?

When the submission of the wife becomes the focus rather than "submitting one to another in the fear of the Lord" (Ephesians 5:21) a distorted picture of submission in marriage results. The husband tends to become domineering, and the wife becomes dominated. Also, this deception implies that a wife is to submit to her husband in doing evil, and that is never to be done. A wife's submission is to be demonstrated by a reverence for her husband as she would have unto the Lord. A husband's submission is to be shown by loving his wife as "Christ also loved the church, and gave himself for it" (Ephesians 5:25–33).

Submission in marriage should be a mutual relationship that is based on a common commitment to Christ.

Submission is a voluntary response of a wife to her husband and is made delightful when he is sacrificially fulfilling the role of Christ in the marriage. Scripture teaches that Godly submission in marriage is a natural result of the following seven focuses.

1. A wife should focus on gratefulness.

In preparation for specific instruction on marriage in the fifth chapter of Ephesians, God gives clear warning that immorality of all kind should "not be once named among you, as becometh saints . . . but rather giving of thanks" (Ephesians 5:3–4).

The command to be thankful is repeated again in one of the verses before discussing the submission of the wife. "Giving thanks always for all things unto God and the Father in the name of our Lord Jesus Christ" (Ephesians 5:20).

A grateful disposition in a wife is a powerful motivation for the husband to honor his wife and revere the Lord, Who is the Source of every good and perfect gift. (See James 1:17.) A wife who is grateful will "reverence her husband" (Ephesians 5:33) for the many positive qualities that he brings to the marriage. This attitude in the wife is a strong motivation for the husband to continue strengthening his positive qualities and working on the negative ones. Simply focusing on submission may result in outward conformity; however, gratefulness is the result of inward devotion. Every husband has a deep need for such devotion and admiration from his wife.

2. A wife should focus on the fear of the Lord.

In Ephesians 5, God precedes His instruction on the marriage relationship with an important mandate to believers, "Submitting yourselves one to another in the fear of God" (Ephesians 5:21).

Submission is a natural result of the reverence that a wife has for the Lord and her husband.

When both partners submit to each other in the fear of the Lord, they will not need to live with the tensions that are implied in this marriage deception. The Lord will convict both the husband and the wife when they are doing wrong.

It is "by the fear of the LORD men depart from evil" (Proverbs 16:6). "The fear of the LORD is the beginning of wisdom" (Proverbs 9:10). "By humility and the fear of the LORD are riches, and honour, and life" (Proverbs 22:4).

The fear of the Lord is the continual awareness that God is watching everything we do, listening to everything we say, and knowing everything that is in our hearts and minds.

When Peter speaks of a wife's submission to her husband, he puts it in the context of the fear of God: "Wives, be in subjection to your own husbands; that, if any obey not the word, they also may without the word be won by the conversation of the wives; While they behold your chaste conversation coupled with fear" (I Peter 3:1–2).

The word *fear* in this passage is the same Greek word as in the Ephesians passage on submitting to one another in the fear of God. (See Ephesians 5:21.)

This attitude of Godly fear and reverence is the focus of walking circumspectly. The fear of God is a tremendous influence on her husband as he sees before him one who has genuine respect, reverence and gratefulness for him. At the same time, this woman is one who has more fear of God than fear of her husband. This enables her to stand for what is right with a right spirit and to not compromise her conscience if she is asked to violate God's Law or act in disobedience to the laws of man that are in accordance with God's Word. God always honors this virtue. "Favour is deceitful, and beauty is vain: but a woman that feareth the LORD, she shall be praised" (Proverbs 31:30).

> *Husbands have a deep desire for reverence from their wives because they know that without it, submission is shallow and insincere.*

3. A wife should focus on reverence.

At the conclusion of the instruction on marriage, Paul states that the wife should "see that she reverence her husband" (Ephesians 5:33).

The Greek word for *reverence* is *phobeo*. It means "in awe of." God tells wives to reverence their husbands because He knows husbands have a deep need and desire for it. They long for honor and reverence because they know that without it, submission is shallow and insincere. Reverence is a matter of the heart, whereas submission is a matter of the mind and the will.

A wife who has a reverent spirit is able to say no to her husband when he asks her to do things that are evil, and he will respect her for her refusal. However, he will tend to react to a wife who may be submissive on the outside but who lacks a spirit of reverence for him.

When a husband does not receive the reverence that he needs from his wife, he will either look for it from other people or attempt to earn it through ambitious schemes that are often ill-conceived. Worse yet, he will just give up and not care what happens.

4. A wife should focus on accountability to God.

The Biblical teaching on submission never allows for a person under authority to do evil. "Servants, be subject to your masters with all fear; not only to the good and gentle, but also to the froward. For this is thankworthy, if a man for conscience toward God endure grief, suffering wrongfully. For what glory is it, if, when ye be buffeted for your faults, ye shall take it patiently? but if, when ye do well, and suffer for it, ye take it patiently, this is acceptable with God. For even hereunto were ye called: because Christ also suffered for us, leaving us an example, that ye should follow his steps: Who did no sin, neither was guile found in his mouth: Who, when he was reviled, reviled not again; when he suffered, he threatened not; but committed himself to him that judgeth righteously" (I Peter 2:18–23).

Sapphira agreed with her husband to lie about the amount they received for the sale of their property and died along with her husband for lying to the Holy Spirit. (See Acts 5:1–2, 8–9).

A wife who demonstrates a spirit of reverence and loyalty toward her husband has the potential for great influence over him.

The Scripture is very clear about personal accountability before God. "For we must all appear before the judgment seat of Christ; that every one may receive the things done in his body, according to that he hath done, whether it be good or bad" (II Corinthians 5:10).

It is vital for a wife to demonstrate a spirit of reverence and loyalty to her husband. If that has not been the case, she should cry out to God for opportunities to show her husband her change of heart. This is crucial if she desires to gain as much influence with her husband as is possible and to be as effective as she could be in coming to him regarding issues in which she could not participate (e.g., illegal or immoral issues).

The need to make a proper disclosure of evil is established in the Law of God. "If a soul sin, and hear the voice of swearing, and is a witness, whether he hath seen or known of it; if he do not utter it, then he shall bear his iniquity" (Leviticus 5:1). To stand by in silence is to be a facilitator of evil and to be equally guilty. One of the grievous examples on this point is when a father or stepfather tragically molests a daughter and the mother allows it to continue by failing to report him to the authorities.

There is further Scripture on this subject: "When I say unto the wicked, Thou shalt surely die; and thou givest him not warning, nor speakest to warn the wicked from his wicked way, to save his life; the same wicked man shall die in his iniquity; but his blood will I require at thine hand" (Ezekiel 3:18).

5. A wife should focus on her position of influence.

In the realm of God-ordained jurisdictions, there are two types of power. First, there is the power of headship, as in the head of state, the head of a family, the head of the Church, and the head of a company. Second, there is the power of influence in those who serve the ones in leadership—the "second in command" and the chief advisors. The record of history and the reality of our observations provide ample confirmation that the greater of these two powers is the power of influence.

The power of influence that is given to a wife is greater than the power of headship that is given to her husband.

When God wants to change the course of history, He often places a man or woman in a position of influence, such as He did with Joseph, Daniel, Esther, and Nehemiah. There are also those who have used their power of influence to impact history in a destructive way. Eve influenced Adam to partake of the forbidden fruit by which sin and death entered into the world and were passed on to all of us. Sarah influenced Abraham to have a child by her servant girl. This initiated the Jewish-Arab conflict, which continues to this very day.

In order for the power of influence to be used effectively, there must be a strong harmony and trust between the one in leadership and the "chief assistant."

6. A wife should focus on her attitude.

Most women acknowledge that their greatest "enemy" is an overwhelming wave of unpredictable emotions. It strongly influences their attitudes and responses to the people and situations around them.

There are physical causes for emotional upheaval in a woman. For this reason, many have said that B-complex vitamins are a husband's best friend. (Along the same lines, B-complex vitamins are a major help in preventing miscarriages.) Besides the physical problems, we must also recognize how the soul functions in order to understand our emotions. The soul is comprised of the mind, will, and emotions. Any two will overcome the third. Thus, if a wife lets her mind think about how her husband has hurt her, and allows her emotions to respond to her thoughts, her determination to keep her vows of marriage may soon be eroded. If, on the other hand, she brings every thought into captivity to the obedience of Christ, and reaffirms the commitment to her vows before God, she will be better able to bring her emotions under control.

When you know a truth that will set a person free and fail to tell it to him or her, you are guilty of the sin of silence.

The wife's goal should be to maintain a spirit of gratefulness and joyfulness. Toward this end, God commands us: "In every thing give thanks: for this is the will of God in Christ Jesus concerning you" (I Thessalonians 5:18), and "Rejoice in the Lord alway: and again I say, Rejoice" (Philippians 4:4).

The gratefulness and joy of a wife and mother empower her husband and family to demonstrate these same qualities. Researchers have discovered that a joyful spirit actually strengthens the immune system and increases health. This is also the message of Scripture: "A merry heart doeth good like a medicine" (Proverbs 17:22), and "The joy of the LORD is your strength" (Nehemiah 8:10).

These qualities are the means by which a husband and wife can escape the destruction of a bitter spirit. Scripture commands husbands not to be bitter toward their wives. "Husbands, love your wives, and be not bitter against them" (Colossians 3:19). We are also warned that through bitterness many are defiled. "Looking diligently lest any man fail of the grace of God; lest any root of bitterness springing up trouble you, and thereby many be defiled" (Hebrews 12:15).

7. A wife should focus on wise appeals.

Wise appeals are powerful. They are so effective that they must be carefully evaluated before they are used, because an appeal for the wrong decision can do great damage.

An appeal is not an attempt by a wife to get her own way but is a well-planned presentation of information to convince her husband that her request will protect his reputation and accomplish the goals that God has for his life, their marriage, and their family. In one sense, the Bible is a "handbook" on how to make wise and effective appeals. It contains many examples of appeals and describes exactly how they were made.

The very prayer that Christ taught His disciples to pray is a masterful appeal. The disciples were first to be concerned for the reputation of their heavenly Father— "Hallowed be thy name." Then, they were to base their requests on His goals, not theirs: "Thy kingdom come." Finally, their appeal was to carry out His will, not theirs. "Thy will be done in earth, as it is in heaven." (See Matthew 6:9–10.)

> *A wife is a helpmeet when she warns her husband that a wrong action will damage his reputation, weaken his authority, and violate God's goals for his life.*

8. A wife should focus on a clear conscience.

Paul sent Timothy out to spiritual warfare with only two weapons—faith and a clear conscience, and without them we could make shipwreck our faith. (See I Timothy 1:19.) When a wife does not have a clear conscience before God and her husband, her past will condemn her and her submission will simply become silent acquiescence to whatever happens. This is not the intended function of a helpmeet or the meaning of submission.

For example, in one marriage, a wife accepted tyrannical domination by her husband because of her guilt in tricking him into marrying her. She viewed his harsh treatment as understandable punishment. Instead, she should have appealed to him for forgiveness.

What are the consequences of this deception?

In the ideal sense, marriage is a relationship that is based on a mutual commitment to Christ in the fear of the Lord. (See Ephesians 5:24.) God designed marriage to be a relationship of joyfulness and fruitfulness. The husband is to see how he can please his wife, and the wife is to see how she can please her husband. (See I Corinthians 7:33–34.)

A false view of submission will also encourage the husband to be his own boss, without accountability for his actions. This domineering husband will forbid his wife to discuss the problems that are in the marriage. This type of husband also rejects the counsel of others who have overcome the problems he is experiencing.

> *A marriage without proper accountability or the ability to make appeals on decisions is tyranny.*

A marriage without proper accountability to higher authorities and without the ability to make wise appeals is a relationship of tyranny. When a wife closes her eyes to wrongdoing that her husband is carrying out, she becomes a facilitator of it. If she cooperates with him, she also is guilty, and exposes her children to risk and possibly to damage.

A husband who is not accountable for his actions develops a hardness of heart. Thus, Scripture commands us to "exhort one another daily, while it is called To-day; lest any of you be hardened through the deceitfulness of sin" (Hebrews 3:13).

A wife who submits to wrongdoing in an effort to hold her marriage together will soon experience destruction to her marriage and see harm done to her sons and daughters.

Why is this deception hard to overcome?

It is difficult to deal with this deception, because it is being promoted by a faulty interpretation of two passages of Scripture. They are both found in the third chapter of first Peter.

The first passage states: "Likewise, ye wives, be in subjection to your own husbands; that, if any obey not the word, they also may without the word be won by the conversation of the wives; While they behold your chaste conversation coupled with fear" (I Peter 3:1–2).

The false idea that is being advocated from these verses is that the wife should win a disobedient husband by silence and good behavior. However, that is not what these verses are stating. The phrase *the word* is referring to the Bible. The Greek word is *logos*— the Word of God. This is not to say that if a husband rejects the Word of God, the wife should not be discouraged—she can win him without the common ground of Biblical instruction. This is not to say that a wife should not discuss Scripture with him, but if he will not receive it, she should focus on her God-given responsibility to fear God, do what is right, revere him in as many areas as possible, and trust God with the results. In the context of the chapter before these verses, they could be read, "In the same way that others with well-doing have put to silence the ignorance of foolish men, wives be subject to your husbands—that if in any area they are disobedient to God's Word, you may win them, without using Scripture, by the influence of your Godly life as you revere your husband and set your heart to do what is right before God."

The second passage follows: "For after this manner in the old time the holy women also, who trusted in God, adorned themselves, being in subjection unto their own husbands: Even as Sarah obeyed Abraham, calling him lord: whose daughters ye are, as long as ye do well, and are not afraid with any amazement" (I Peter 3:5 7).

Against this background, many proponents of unquestioning obedience then go to the account of Sarah's obedience to Abraham in lying about her position as his wife.

When Abraham came to the land of King Abimelech, he assumed that the fear of God was not among those people, so he feared that the king would kill him in order to take away his wife Sarah, who was very beautiful. So he and Sarah agreed together to lie about their relationship as husband and wife.

Sarah is a role model to be followed for submission, but only as long as the wife does that which is good.

When King Abimelech discovered that Abraham and Sarah had lied to him, he reproved Abraham by saying, "What hast thou done unto us? and what have I offended thee, that thou hast brought on me and on my kingdom a great sin? thou hast done deeds unto me that ought not to be done" (Genesis 20:9).

Then Abimelech reproved Sarah for agreeing to the lie. "And unto Sarah he said, Behold, I have given thy brother a thousand pieces of silver: behold, he is to thee a covering of the eyes, unto all that are with thee, and with all other: thus she was reproved" (Genesis 20:16).

The Hebrew word for *reproved (yakach)* can mean "to be made right." However, this does not refer to Sarah's lie, but in her being made right as a wife. Abimelech was saying, "Act like a married woman, and wear your veil."

> *Reverence comes by distinguishing between a husband's God-given position and his human personality.*

Lying is a serious offense. Jesus said to the Pharisees, "Ye are of your father the devil . . . When he speaketh a lie, he speaketh of his own: for he is a liar, and the father of it" (John 8:44). And Revelation 21:8 says "all liars, shall have their part in the lake which burneth with fire and brimstone."

Sapphira was condemned to death for agreeing with her husband to lie about how much money they received from the sale of their property. Why, then, should Sarah be vindicated for telling her lie, which jeopardized a righteous man's position and brought his whole kingdom under God's judgment?

Further translations of the Hebrew word *yakach* are *chasten, rebuke,* and *reprove. Reprove* is used in the following passages.

- "These things hast thou done, and I kept silence; thou thoughtest that I was altogether such an one as thyself: but I will reprove [*yakach*] thee, and set them in order before thine eyes" (Psalm 50:21).

- "Add thou not unto his words, lest he reprove [*yakach*] thee, and thou be found a liar" (Proverbs 30:6).

This is not the first time that Sarah had lied. When the Lord visited Abraham and told him that Sarah would have a child, she overheard their announcement and "laughed within herself" (Genesis 18:12). When the Lord asked Abraham why his wife laughed, "Sarah denied, saying, I laughed not; for she was afraid. And he said, Nay; but thou didst laugh" (Genesis 18:15).

The deception of Abraham and Sarah had serious consequences in the iniquities that were passed on to their descendants. Isaac had his wife Rebekah repeat the same lie in a similar circumstance. (See Genesis 25.) Then their son Jacob deceived Isaac by claiming to be the firstborn, Esau (see Genesis 27:19.), and Jacob's sons deceived Jacob with the bloody coat of Joseph. (See Genesis 37:31–32.)

Notice that the passage in I Peter about Sarah obeying Abraham refers only to the submission of a wife "as long as you do well"— it is not for doing evil, such as lying or being immoral. Also, the Biblical reference to Sarah calling Abraham "lord" is not related to the account of her deception as to their relationship but to having a son in old age. "After I am waxed old shall I have pleasure, my lord being old also?" (Genesis 18:12).

Principles of a Wise Appeal

Many appeals are not effective because they violate one or more of the following guidelines for an effective appeal. All seven points should be in an appeal. Often, a wife's appeal is rejected because her husband senses one of these points is missing. A proper appeal is really an exercise in reverence. In order to properly appeal, we must keep watch over our mouths.

1. Be in "right standing."

To be in right standing, the wife must be in harmony with her husband, and also with the Lord. She must be committed to her husband, whatever his failures and shortcomings, so that his heart "safely trusts in her." (See Proverbs 31:11.) If she has developed an independent spirit or resistant attitude in her relationship to him and to his authority, her appeal will probably be viewed as a further expression of self-will and will not be heard.

The motive of an appeal should be to honor the reputation, goals, and authority of the one we are serving.

When Daniel made an appeal to the king's official for a menu that would not violate his Biblical convictions, he first established the fact that he and his companions were servants of the king. "Prove thy servants, I beseech thee, ten days; and let them give us pulse to eat, and water to drink" (Daniel 1:12). Even the donkey that refused to follow the directives of its erring rider declared her right standing in the appeal by reminding Balaam that she had always been obedient to him in every other matter since the day she began serving him. (See Numbers 22:30.)

2. Have the right motives.

Those in authority usually realize the importance of their reputation, since "a good name is rather to be chosen than great riches" (Proverbs 22:1). When a husband wants to do wrong, his wife's first concern should be to protect his name and reputation.

Moses turned God's wrath away from the nation of Israel by appealing to God's reputation. He "reminded" God that if He destroyed the Israelites it would bring damage to His name. "I prayed therefore unto the LORD, and said, O Lord GOD, destroy not thy people and thine inheritance which thou hast redeemed through thy greatness . . . Lest the land whence thou broughtest us out say, Because the LORD was not able to bring them into the land which he promised them, and because he hated them, he hath brought them out to slay them in the wilderness" (Deuteronomy 9:26–28).

Esther used the power of curiosity to gain the attention of the king for an appeal.

Having the right motives involves a genuine concern for the work and reputation of the Lord and the success and welfare of your spouse. A powerful basis of right motives is given in the prayer that Jesus taught us to use. "After this manner therefore pray ye: Our Father which art in heaven, Hallowed be thy name. Thy kingdom come. Thy will be done in earth, as it is in heaven" (Matthew 6:9–10).

Notice the three motives of this appeal. First is a concern for the reputation of the Lord—"Hallowed be thy name." Next, there is the motive of fulfilling His goals—"Thy kingdom come." The third motive is a desire to honor His leadership—"Thy will be done."

A wife must also know the goals and objectives of her husband and explain how a wrong decision will damage or violate these goals. A further motive would be to appeal to the husband's authority and responsibility to protect his wife, family, and assets. One of the strongest ways to appeal to a man is to activate his protective instincts.

In order to carry out this requirement, it is important for the wife to find out what her husband's goals and objectives are for his life and for their marriage and family. Many times, the husband will not have identified these in his own mind. A wise wife will help him clarify them and then be committed to helping him reach them.

3. Choose the right timing.

The appeal of Queen Esther to the king is a marvelous example of choosing the right timing. She knew that the king had many other concerns on his mind and would not be able to give the required attention to her appeal. Therefore, she made careful preparations both spiritually and physically to have the appeal come at just the right time. Her preparations involved a three-day fast and then an invitation for the king to come to a special dinner to hear her appeal. At this dinner and a subsequent one, she had his full attention and appreciation, and her appeal was heard and granted.

It is wise for a wife to use discernment, ask the Lord for right timing, and then ask her husband, "Is this a good time to discuss an important matter?" This is important because when a husband's mind is on many other concerns, he may hear the words of an appeal but not comprehend their significance or his need to act upon them.

4. Give accurate information.

In order for the husband to make a wise decision, he must have all the facts that are related to it. A husband will know if his wife is unaware of important facts or is ignoring them. This may influence him to have a negative outlook toward her appeal. The very reason that he is making a wrong decision is often a result of a lack of information, misinformation, or strongholds in his mind that must be cast down. His wife must give him her perspective with facts that he may have overlooked.

Often a wife will not be able to give the specific reasons why a decision is wrong; nevertheless, God will give her clear cautions that the husband does not have. If the husband neglects or overrides these cautions, he will not be respecting the value the Lord placed in his wife nor the warnings that the Lord is giving him through her and will receive the reproofs of life for doing so.

More appeals are probably rejected because of wrong attitudes than for any other reason.

Giving accurate information also involves presenting it with appropriate emotions. If something is very serious, the emotions should reflect that fact. However, if there is great agitation in the wife over a minor matter, the husband will tend to react to the emotions and not respond to any of her appeals.

5. Have the right attitudes.

Probably more appeals are rejected because of wrong attitudes than for any other reason. The attitude of a wife must include loyalty, gratefulness, and reverence. If the husband senses disloyalty, ungratefulness, or disrespect, he will probably not even hear the appeal. He will tend to react to these negative attitudes and be more concerned about them than her appeal.

It would be appropriate for the wife to begin her appeal by affirming her commitment to her husband and doing all she can to make him successful.

Gratefulness is expressed by recalling the sacrifices that he has made for her and the family. It is destroyed by focusing on expectations. Unfulfilled expectations, if not responded to properly, result in a wounded spirit, which acts like a poison.

The gracious words of a wife's appeal motivate the husband to do what is right.

An expectation is a mental obligation that we assign to another person. When a spouse fulfills an expectation, we tend to be ungrateful since we believe it was owed to us. If the expectation is not fulfilled, we tend to become bitter and resentful, believing we were cheated. Expectations turn loved ones into prisoners. This is especially true with family members, since we tend to expect more from them than from other people. It is often for this reason that we tend to get along better with people who are outside of the family.

Reverence comes by separating an authority's divine position from his personality. A wife communicates reverence by assuring him that God's pattern is to lead the family through the husband.

6. Use appropriate words.

A wife may have the right standing, the right motives, the right timing, the right information, and the right attitudes but fail to choose the words that convey what she really means.

Usually, the very nature of any appeal is going to go against the intentions of the authority. The wife's appeal will usually be contrary to the will and plans of the husband and, therefore, can be easily misunderstood. It is extremely important for a wife to choose words that will guide her appeal around the mental roadblocks of her husband.

The test of an appeal is purposing to thank God, whether it is accepted or rejected.

Right words are gracious words, they are humble words, and they are accurate words. They must not be inflammatory. A wife also uses right wording when she presents her appeal from the husband's point of view rather than her own perspective.

To avoid unnecessary reaction, choose words that will guide important ideas around the mental roadblocks of a husband. Proverbs emphasizes the importance of using right words when appealing to one in authority. "He that loveth pureness of heart, for the grace of his lips the king shall be his friend" (Proverbs 22:11). A further encouragement for using right words is the following instruction: "Let your speech be alway with grace, seasoned with salt, that ye may know how ye ought to answer every man" (Colossians 4.6).

Gracious words would therefore energize a husband to do what is right. The seasoning of salt brings out taste and creates thirst. The words of a wife can be very effective in creating curiosity in her husband, as well as the motivation to act upon it.

A further aspect of right wording is for the wife to explain the personal sacrifice that she is willing to make in order for her appeal to be accepted. When a husband realizes the extent to which his wife is willing to make sacrifices for her appeal, he is highly motivated to respond positively to it.

7. Prepare a right response.

If the appeal is righteous and if the wife gives it in a proper way, it is the Lord's responsibility to work in the heart of her husband, because "the king's heart is in the hand of the LORD, as the rivers of water: he turneth it whithersoever he will" (Proverbs 21:1). Unless the appeal requires an immediate decision, it is important for the wife to give time for God to continue working on her husband's heart. When an appeal is heard, the wife should demonstrate sincere gratefulness to her husband. This will build a further bonding for communication and oneness of spirit in the marriage.

Confirming Testimonies

How a Wife's Silence Resulted in Tragic Consequences

On our wedding day, my husband and I made a vow to love and cherish one another until death parted us. Now twenty-five years later we are another divorce statistic. Where did we go wrong?

We fell prey to Satan's deception. My husband believed that lust and pornography would not affect his wife, children, or ministry. He lived the life of a hypocrite. Satan's deception led him to believe that only his "talk" mattered, not his "walk." He thought he could "control" his lust problem, but the little bit of "leaven" he allowed in his life leavened the whole lump. In time, his heart was completely hardened against God's truth, and he fell into gross immorality.

What was my response as I saw my husband drift further and further away from God? Initially I made excuses for my husband, or I blamed myself, "Maybe the problem was overwork or depression; if only I had been more submissive." So I quietly accepted my situation. This year, my eyes were opened to Satan's deadly deceptions. I gained a new understanding of God's Word, which gave me peace and quiet from Satan's accusations.

As I saw my husband slipping away from God, I appealed to him, but he angrily condemned me for my lack of submission and respect. I felt lonely and rejected. Now I understand the oneness I craved was impossible because he did not cherish me and did not save himself for me only. Through the years, because I did not have all of his heart, I felt a lack of acceptance. Every human heart longs for acceptance. This lack of acceptance provoked me to outbursts of anger, which left me feeling guilty and defeated.

My first deception was believing that any further appeals would be unsubmissive—if I spoke to my husband about his sin. After appealing to my husband about his broken marriage vow and how this would damage not only his family but the many people he had worked so hard to spiritually encourage, he responded by making false promises: saying that when he had less pressure he would get marriage counseling. Here was another deception. Because I didn't have a better understanding of sin—that without true repentance sin never gets better, it always gets worse—I compromised my whole family by not seeking help from my husband's authorities, who had a heart for us and could have helped.

I now understand the dangerous potential of sin, if not dealt with immediately, to damage a marriage, a family, a ministry, or a life. I should have acted with urgency and gone for counsel and help. I thought things would "work out" as our circumstances improved. Oh, if only I had had a greater fear of God and evil, but I did not understand the whole counsel of the Scriptures and I blindly followed the misquoted Scripture, "Wives, win your husbands without a word." I longed to go to the Body of Christ for help but condemned myself for having a lack of faith in God and having an unsubmissive heart.

Because of my despair over my husband's open rejection of me, he agreed to have me counsel with two Christian authors. Both advised that I would be unsubmissive to my husband and not receive God's blessing if I went against my husband's wishes by appealing to his authorities. My silence was an incubator for my husband's sins to grow out of control. This deception was the deadliest of all. Scripture says that "my people perish for lack of knowledge."

I rejoice to now take hold of God's precious truth and reach out to all in my sphere of influence to expose this deception. We can guard against error by knowing truth because it will set us free, by being accountable to the Body of Christ, by exhorting one another daily, and by fleeing from evil. I trust that in obedience to His Word and with repentance God will give me beauty for ashes.

—A hopeful wife

How Telling the Whole Truth
Gave a Wife a Whole New Value

Thank you, Mike and Connie, for another inspiring conference. A burden has been lifted! Your session helped me overcome a major guilt problem. In the past I interpreted most of the marriage teaching on submission as "put up and shut up." I thought I was only to appeal on very important matters, and if my husband didn't listen, I was to be a joyful, submissive wife, trusting in God while watching my husband jump off a cliff and take the rest of us with him. There was no joy in my attitude.

I just couldn't hold my cautions in without becoming bitter and resentful and wondered why the great fulfillment in marriage eluded me. I was told that a wife's greatest need was communication, yet I was not allowed to fulfill this need. When I would read books that had the "put up and shut up" mentality, I was saddened. I chided myself that I was just a rebellious, independent wife who had to get her "two cents" in.

I even felt badly for expressing myself in a respectful way. I also sensed I was of little use to my husband and that I contributed little to the marriage.

Another dimension that added to my guilt was the fact my husband has a background that emphasizes the male leadership and the female submission. This is Scriptural truth that can easily be taken out of balance.

Now as I look back, my cautions have helped my husband, and he acknowledges this too. I realize also, that cautions can be misused, but this is not my intent. I just needed to be encouraged that gently warning my husband is not wrong when done with a right attitude, right words, and right timing. In fact, these cautions are intended to bring us together in oneness. Now I realize that I am a valuable asset to my husband, not simply a maid. Realizing that I hold a position that no one else on earth can fulfill has given me great worth. I now understand what my design as this "help" is! Thank you for clearing up this teaching in my mind!

—A joyful wife

How a Husband Determined to Pay Any Price When He Found the Right Example

When Mike and Connie began their presentation, I was somewhat skeptical. Then I noticed how Connie was standing beside Mike, looking attentively at him. Her countenance reflected peace, joy, respect, honor, and reverence. I purposed that if what they were going to say would allow my wife to look at me the way Connie looked at Mike, no matter what they said, no matter what it took, no matter what it cost, I would do it!

—A resolute husband

Evaluation for the Husband

1. Do you expect your wife to obey you whether you are right or wrong?

1 2 3 4 5 6 7 8 9 10
Always   Never

2. Do you use outbursts of anger to control or intimidate your wife?

1 2 3 4 5 6 7 8 9 10
Always   Never

3. Would your wife say that you have an attitude of pride and domination?

1 2 3 4 5 6 7 8 9 10
Always   Never

4. Do you tend to reject your wife when you do not agree with her?

1 2 3 4 5 6 7 8 9 10
Always   Never

5. Have you made your wife's submission your focus rather than your own to the Lord?

1 2 3 4 5 6 7 8 9 10
Never   Always

6. Do you take your wife's concerns to the Lord in prayer and seek His direction?

1 2 3 4 5 6 7 8 9 10
Never   Always

7. Do you react to your wife's appeals as attempts to manipulate you?

1 2 3 4 5 6 7 8 9 10
Always   Never

8. Would you say that your wife demonstrated that her ultimate desire is to do good to you?

1 2 3 4 5 6 7 8 9 10
Never   Always

Oh Lord, forgive me for distorting Your design for submission by using it as a way to control my wife. I now repent of the anger and pride that I have used to dominate her. I do purpose to listen to my wife's concerns and share them with You. You designed me, as her husband, to love her as Christ loved us and gave Himself for us. I do recognize that I am not to demand submission, but to be an example to her of it by how I submit to Christ.

Date prayed: _____   Initials _____

Evaluation for the Wife

1. Would your husband say that you have a grateful and joyful spirit?

   1 2 3 4 5 6 7 8 9 10
   Never   Always

2. Do you encourage a fear of the Lord by asking your husband what God would think about a matter?

   1 2 3 4 5 6 7 8 9 10
   Never   Always

3. How sincere would your husband say that your reverence is toward him?

   1 2 3 4 5 6 7 8 9 10
   Neglect   Excellent

4. Are you able to separate your husband's God-given position from his personality?

   1 2 3 4 5 6 7 8 9 10
   Never   Always

5. Have you purposed to appeal to your husband whenever he asks you to do something wrong?

   1 2 3 4 5 6 7 8 9 10
   Never   Always

6. Are you able to discern when to appeal and when to be patient?

   1 2 3 4 5 6 7 8 9 10
   Never   Always

7. Have you focused on maintaining a clear conscience before God and your husband?

   1 2 3 4 5 6 7 8 9 10
   Never   Always

8. Have you purposed to follow the seven steps of making a wise appeal?

   1 2 3 4 5 6 7 8 9 10
   Never   Always

O Lord, forgive me for believing the deception that it is not my responsibility to warn my husband of danger. I reject the lie that somehow I will escape the consequences for his behavior by concentrating on my life before You. I realize now that the Biblical concept of oneness means I share in his successes as well as his failures. I accept my responsibility to warn him using wise appeals.

Date prayed: _____   Initials _____

Chapter Six

Deception Number Six:

"If a husband rejects his wife's appeal, she should simply pray."

Why is this a deception?

The statement that a wife should simply pray if her appeal is rejected assumes that her appeal was right and should have been granted and that her only responsibility is to ask God to change her husband's heart. This fails to identify the further steps she should take to evaluate her methods and motives in appealing and her responsibility to take the most serious matters to higher authorities.

1. Was the appeal wisely designed?

Medical doctors tend to react to patients who tell them what to do. Instead, doctors want their patients to tell them their symptoms; then they will make a diagnosis and recommend the treatment that they believe will be most effective. It may be that the patient actually knows of a better treatment than the doctor; however, it is still wise to begin by identifying the symptoms, so that together a correct diagnosis can be made and the best treatment followed.

A husband tends to respond the same way when his wife tells him what to do in an appeal. Instead of giving direction, it would be wise for the wife to identify the symptoms of the problem, and then the

> *An appeal by the wife should not make the husband feel as though the decision has already been made.*

husband and wife can arrive at a correct diagnosis and seek the Lord for the best course of action.

For example, a wife may appeal to her husband to send their wayward son to a private school. Such an appeal is jumping to a treatment without first analyzing the symptoms and the diagnosis. Are the parents dealing with a son who is into addictions, frustrated, peer dependent, bitter, a slow learner, or just plain rebellious? How will the school deal with the particular problems that he has?

Prayer is not something to be done only after an appeal but before it is given.

2. Was the appeal preceded by prayer?

The deceptive statement communicates the idea that prayer should only follow an appeal. Instead, it should precede the appeal. The statement also suggests that prayer is somewhat less effective than the wife's appeal. However, when "effectual, fervent prayer" precedes an appeal, much power is made available. (See James 5:16.)

Before Queen Esther made her appeal to King Ahasuerus, she and her maidens and all the Jews in the city fasted and prayed for three days and three nights. (See Esther 4:16.) Jesus promised that if we fast and pray secretly, we will be rewarded openly. (See Matthew 6:17–18.)

Through our spending time in prayer and fasting before making an appeal, the Lord is able to refine our attitudes, thoughts, motives, and emotions. Then our trust in the Lord's ability to work out His will in the response to our appeal will increase, since "the king's heart is in the hand of the LORD, as the rivers of water: he turneth it whithersoever he will" (Proverbs 21:1).

Fasting greatly increases spiritual perception and allows us to see God's perspective on the pressures and problems we face. Before Nehemiah made his appeal to the king whom he served, he too spent several days in earnest fasting and prayer. "It came to pass, when I heard these words, that I sat down and wept, and mourned certain days, and fasted, and prayed before the God of heaven" (Nehemiah 1:4). The importance of fasting should not be minimized. When directed by the Lord, even a brief period of fasting (i.e., for a meal or two) can be a critical element in seeing God's purposes accomplished.

3. Was the appeal made with gratefulness?

The importance of adding a spirit of gratefulness to an appeal is emphasized in the following passage: "Be careful for nothing; but in every thing by prayer and supplication with thanksgiving let your requests be made known unto God. And the peace of God, which passeth all understanding, shall keep your hearts and minds through Christ Jesus" (Philippians 4:6–7).

Every appeal must be presented in a spirit of gratefulness for what has already been done for us. Gratefulness gives energy to the one who receives our appeal, whereas a lack of gratefulness drains energy and creates a spirit of reaction in the one receiving the appeal.

4. Was the appeal well thought-out?

After Esther gained the full attention of the king, he said to her, "What is thy petition, queen Esther? and it shall be granted thee: and what is thy request? and it shall be performed, even to the half of the kingdom" (Esther 7:2). Esther responded, "If I have found favour in thy sight, O king, and if it please the king, let my life be given me at my petition, and my people at my request" (Esther 7:3).

Esther had carefully laid the groundwork for the king to grant her appeal, even before she gave it. The appeal itself was actually for the benefit of the king and not for her, as she points out: "If we had been sold for bondmen and bondwomen, I had held my tongue, although the enemy could not countervail the king's damage" (Esther 7:4).

During her time of prayer and fasting, Esther carefully thought through her appeal.

A carefully thought-out appeal will be recognized by the one being appealed to as a benefit to him and his program, rather than for the selfish indulgence of the one making the appeal. God makes the same requirements for appeals that we make to him. "Ye have not, because ye ask not. Ye ask, and receive not, because ye ask amiss, that ye may consume it upon your lusts" (James 4:2–3).

5. Does the appeal allow time for evaluation?

Solomon observed that "by long forbearing is a prince persuaded, and a soft tongue breaketh the bone" (Proverbs 25:15). If an appeal requires a major change in planning, ideas, or direction, it will take time for the one hearing the appeal to rethink his conclusions in these areas.

A wife who makes an appeal to her husband must give God time to change his mind. Those who wait until the last minute to present their ideas and expect an immediate response create unnecessary pressure and build up resistance for this and future appeals. Rushed appeals also cut out time to seek the Lord's will.

What are the consequences of this deception?

If a wife has the attitude that all of her appeals are right, there will be no rest or resolution until she gets what she asked for. If the husband rejects her appeals, she will make him feel that he must now deal with God, Who is "obviously on her side."

This may well be the case in certain situations, yet there will be others in which a "no" should bring the matter to a close, and still other situations in which the wife must do more than "just pray."

1. Should the appeal be repeated?

If the husband rejects a correct appeal made by the wife, it is the Lord who will then put pressure on him rather than the wife.

The Apostle Paul appealed to God three times to have a "thorn in the flesh" removed from him. "I besought the Lord thrice, that it might depart from me" (II Corinthians 12:8); only after the third time did he understand why his appeal was turned down. God's "better idea" transformed his infirmity into a source of spiritual power. "And he said unto me, My grace is sufficient for thee: for my strength is made perfect in weakness. Most gladly therefore will I rather glory in my infirmities, that the power of Christ may rest upon me" (II Corinthians 12:9).

Jesus commended the widow for "her continual coming" to the unjust judge. (See Luke 18:5.) She was in urgent need of justice, and the unjust judge was the only one who could give it. "And he would not for a while: but afterward he said within himself, Though I fear not God, nor regard man; Yet because this widow troubleth me, I will avenge her, lest by her continual coming she weary me.

And the Lord said, Hear what the unjust judge saith. And shall not God avenge his own elect, which cry day and night unto him, though he bear long with them? I tell you that he will avenge them speedily. Nevertheless when the Son of man cometh, shall he find faith on the earth?" (Luke 18:4–8).

When the laws of God or man are broken by a husband who rejects every appeal, the appeal must be taken to higher authorities.

In order for a wife to repeat her appeal, she must be confident that it is right and consistent with the will of God. Pilate's wife made an appeal to him to not condemn Jesus because He was an innocent man. Her appeal was correct; however, it was not in harmony with the greater purposes of God for the death, burial, and resurrection of Christ.

If a wife's appeal is not urgent or concerning a major matter, she should not repeat her appeal lest she be seen as a "continual dripping." "A continual dropping in a very rainy day and a contentious woman are alike" (Proverbs 27:15). "It is better to dwell in the wilderness, than with a contentious and an angry woman" (Proverbs 21:19).

2. Should the appeal be taken higher?

If the purpose of the wife's appeal is to stop or avoid abuse to her or the children, it must be taken to higher authorities. The first authority to be called in should be the wife's father, if he is available, since he was the one who entrusted her to the care and protection of her husband.

The second level would be church authorities. They are responsible for the spiritual welfare of both the husband and the wife. "Obey them that have the rule over you, and submit yourselves: for they watch for your souls, as they that must give account, that they may do it with joy, and not with grief: for that is unprofitable for you" (Hebrews 13:17). If the wrongdoing of the husband involves only spiritual matters, church authorities should be able to deal with the situation. However, if the law has been broken, they must transfer the matter to proper government authorities.

When serious appeals from the wife are rejected by a husband, it may well be that she is not the one who should be talking with him. If laws are being broken and she simply prays about the matter, the consequences of his actions will damage her and the family.

Law officers are ministers of God for doing good. They are a terror to evil workers and a protector of those who do good.

3. Should the appeal be dropped?

If an appeal does not fall within the first two categories, then the answer of the husband should be final. The wife's attitude at this point will be an important indicator of her faith and a testimony to her husband. It should involve the following five factors:

There is a special energy that comes from a grateful person that makes the appeal more effective and likely to be heard.

1. Choose to be grateful.

When we do not get what we request, our natural response is to murmur and complain. However, if we want to experience the power of God's Spirit (love, joy, and peace), we must have an opposite response. Instead of being disappointed or angry, we must choose to be grateful. This is consistent with God's instruction, "In every thing give thanks: for this is the will of God in Christ Jesus concerning you" (I Thessalonians 5:18).

There are solid, Biblical reasons why we can sincerely thank God "in all things." First, everything that happens to us comes from the direct or permissive hand of God and is designed for our good. This is the assurance of Scripture: "And we know that all things work together for good to them that love God, to them who are the called according to his purpose" (Romans 8:28). The following verse explains how they work together for our good—they conform us to the character of Christ. (See Romans 8:29.)

An example of this truth is when Pharaoh rejected the appeal of God through Moses to let His people go: God hardened Pharaoh's heart and used his harsh treatment to build up the people so that when Pharaoh commanded them to leave Egypt, they went with riches, and "there was not one feeble person among their tribes" (Psalm 105:37). This is true in every situation. This is the marvelous hope of all believers.

2. Find reasons to rejoice.

Not only are we to be thankful with our emotions, but we are to rejoice in our spirits. "Rejoice in the Lord alway: and again I say,

Rejoice" (Philippians 4:4). In order to rejoice, we need to find benefits that we can rejoice over.

It is easy to think of the benefits of getting what we asked for. However, it is equally important to think of benefits for not getting what we wanted. A philosopher once observed that there are two tragedies in life. One is not getting what we want, and the other is getting what we want. The point is that we do not always know what is best for us. However, God does. "No good thing will he withhold from them that walk uprightly" (Psalm 84:11).

An example of this is what happened to a minister when he arrived at an airport about ten minutes before his plane was to leave—the door was already closed, and the plane was pulling away from the gate. He appealed to the supervisor to let him get on that plane, because he had a speaking engagement that night. The supervisor told him that even though his ticket indicated he was there on time, they could not pull the plane back and he would have to take the next flight.

The most important reasons to rejoice are the specific character qualities that we can learn by responding to the acceptance or rejection of an appeal.

The minister sat down to wait, and in a short while the airline supervisor came to him and asked, "Why are you not angry?" He explained that he belonged to the Lord and that his schedule was under God's control. If God wanted him on that plane, He would have held it there until the departure time or He would have moved in the heart of the supervisor to call the plane back.

A short time later, the airline supervisor came over to the minister and informed him that the plane he was scheduled to fly out on had crashed and that there were no survivors. The minister's first response to having his appeal rejected should have been to thank God, and now he had reasons to do so.

Sometimes the benefits of having the appeal rejected are not readily seen. However, there are always character qualities—such as patience, self-control, flexibility, endurance, and resourcefulness—that will be developed through a proper response to a disappointment. These are some of the benefits that are cause for rejoicing.

3. Search for rhemas.

One of God's purposes in allowing us to experience problems is for us to find and live out the Scripture that relates to them. For example, if we go through the pain of rejection, we will find great comfort, encouragement, and direction in specific Psalms and other passages. By internalizing these Scriptures, we become living epistles of God's Word, and when the trials are over, we have rich counsel and comfort to give to others who go through similar problems. It is on the basis of these Scriptures that we are to make appeals to God and others.

Only as we have faith in the power and working of the Lord in our trials will we have the ability to "rejoice evermore" (I Thessalonians 5:16). This kind of faith comes by engrafting these special passages of Scripture into our minds, wills, and emotions. Such passages become *rhema*s [Greek: utterance] from the Bible. They are given to us by the Holy Spirit for our personal application. "So then faith cometh by hearing, and hearing by the word [*rhema*] of God" (Romans 10:17).

> *Rhemas are the passages of Scripture that the Holy Spirit uses to give us direction or understanding.*

When Jesus was first tempted by Satan in the wilderness, Jesus answered with a rhema that He had received from His Heavenly Father. The very rhema He used spoke of the power and importance of rhemas. "And the devil said unto him, If thou be the Son of God, command this stone that it be made bread. And Jesus answered him, saying, It is written, That man shall not live by bread alone, but by every word [*rhema*] of God" (Luke 4:3–4).

As the Holy Spirit illuminates a passage of Scripture to us, we should write it out, memorize it, and meditate on it. We can then use these Scriptures in our appeals to the Lord. "If ye abide in me, and my words [*rhema*] abide in you, ye shall ask what ye will, and it shall be done unto you" (John 15:7).

4. Cry out for deliverance from troubles.

Much frustration, discouragement, and defeat can be avoided in the Christian life if we understand that God will often put us in impossible situations. His purpose is to have us realize that we cannot solve these problems or change the hearts of people with our own energies or abilities. Instead, He wants us to cry out to Him, and then He will deliver us so that we can glorify Him. This is the promise of Psalm 50:15: "And call upon me in the day of trouble: I will deliver thee, and thou shalt glorify me."

This pattern of trouble, crying out, deliverance, and glorifying God is illustrated throughout Scripture but is summarized in Psalm 107. Four times in this chapter there are trials and troubles, and four times there is deliverance—but only when those in distress cry out. The following is the fourth example:

"For he commandeth, and raiseth the stormy wind, which lifteth up the waves thereof. They mount up to the heaven, they go down again to the depths: their soul is melted because of trouble. They reel to and fro, and stagger like a drunken man, and are at their wit's end. Then they cry unto the LORD in their trouble, and he bringeth them out of their distresses. He maketh the storm a calm, so that the waves thereof are still. Then are they glad because they be quiet; so he bringeth them unto their desired haven. Oh that men would praise the LORD for his goodness, and for his wonderful works to the children of men!" (Psalm 107:25–31).

When a wife has made a proper appeal to her husband on a serious matter that she believes to be God's will, and he does not respond positively to it, she should get alone with the Lord and cry out for God to carry out His will in this matter.

> *God designed the Christian life to be impossible so that we would have to cry out for His power, provision, protection, and direction on a regular basis.*

5. Overcome evil with good works.

The appeals that we make should not be for our own personal gain but to make us more effective in benefiting the lives of others and advancing the work of the Lord. It is for this purpose that we are redeemed by the blood of the Lord Jesus Christ, "Who gave himself for us, that he might redeem us from all iniquity, and purify unto himself a peculiar people, zealous of good works" (Titus 2:14).

Carrying out good works is a powerful response in overcoming evil. "Be not overcome of evil, but overcome evil with good"

(Romans 12:21). Whatever the response is to our appeals, we should continue to be zealous of good works.

The Rewards of Rejoicing in Trials

1. The Power of Genuine Love

"And not only so, but we glory in tribulations also: knowing that tribulation worketh patience; And patience, experience; and experience, hope: And hope maketh not ashamed; because the love of God is shed abroad in our hearts by the Holy Ghost which is given unto us" (Romans 5:3–5).

2. The Power of Exceeding Joy

"Beloved, think it not strange concerning the fiery trial which is to try you, as though some strange thing happened unto you: But rejoice, inasmuch as ye are partakers of Christ's sufferings; that, when his glory shall be revealed, ye may be glad also with exceeding joy" (I Peter 4:12–13).

3. The Power of God's Glory

"If ye be reproached for the name of Christ, happy are ye; for the spirit of glory and of God resteth upon you: on their part he is evil spoken of, but on your part he is glorified" (I Peter 4:14).

There are three stages in the believer's life. First is the indwelling and filling of the Spirit, second is the testing of the Spirit, and third is the power of the Spirit.

4. The Power of Christ

"That Christ may dwell in your hearts by faith; that ye, being rooted and grounded in love, May be able to comprehend with all saints what is the breadth, and length, and depth, and height; And to know the love of Christ, which passeth knowledge, that ye might be filled with all the fulness of God. Now unto him that is able to do exceeding abundantly above all that we ask or think, according to the power that worketh in us" (Ephesians 3:17).

5. The Resurrection Power of Christ

"Yea doubtless, and I count all things but loss for the excellency of the knowledge of Christ Jesus my Lord: for whom I have suffered the loss of all things, and do count them but dung, that I may win Christ, And be found in him, not having mine own righteousness, which is of the law, but that which is through the faith of Christ, the righteousness which is of God by faith: That I may know him, and the power of his resurrection, and the fellowship of his sufferings, being made conformable unto his death" (Philippians 3:8–10).

> *The power of God's Spirit includes the fruit of the Spirit, beginning with love, joy, and peace.*

Confirming Testimony

How a Husband Learned to Appreciate the Innate Business Skills of His Wife

My husband is self-employed and was developing a second, home-based business that our older children would enjoy working together in. He was talking in the evenings with them: planning and developing the business. As a result, he had been neglecting our special evening times talking to me, which I so looked forward to. I asked, "Could we have some time together?" He agreed but said, "For now we have to wait."

A couple of months passed. We needed to discuss other family matters: issues with younger children, house repairs, schooling issues, etc., but he had too much on his mind, and all my requests seemed to go in one ear and out the other.

Then I began having troubling thoughts of the new business. I knew he would view my thoughts as rejection and criticism. I tested the waters by asking some pointed questions about the business. He responded sarcastically by asking, "What do you know about business math?"

Amazingly I didn't react! Instead, I reviewed the steps of an effective appeal (Chapter 5) and began writing out an appeal I knew I needed to make. I carefully followed the steps outlined and step by step prepared my appeal from his perspective. I sensed a blindness in my husband by this new business opportunity. At the same time I was alarmed at his seeming dullness for not thinking the whole thing through. I knew I would need God to go before me. As a wife, this was a fearful place to be in, knowing your husband is making decisions that the whole family will suffer for. I fasted for three days and cried out to God! Scripture just jumped off the page, during this time, about this situation.

I knew my attitude would play such an important part in my appeal. The thought hit me, "Will you be able to thank God if he rejects it?" After some soul-searching, I finally could say, "Yes, we are in this together—thick or thin, for better or for worse. We have fallen on hard times before." I assured myself we could make it. I prepared myself for the adjustments that would need to be made if my appeal was rejected.

Hoping for the best, I approached him. All went well until he threw a new twist into the discussion that I wasn't prepared for. I got all emotional. He rejected my appeal. I felt like I had failed. Defeated, I crawled into bed that night thinking, "Lord, teach me Your will; I delight to do Your will!"

The next day, I knew discouragement would hit hard if I didn't have something to hope in. "God, where are You in all of this?" I read a Psalm. "Why are you cast down, oh my soul? Hope in God: for I shall yet praise Him for the help of His countenance." I prayed, "God, I need to see You in this decision. Help me have a right attitude!" Each day I purposed to look for something good to carry me through.

They were small things. One day it was faith of a "mustard seed" to remove obstacles. Another day it was gratefulness for things I took for granted. Yet another day it was resourcefulness, realizing how wasteful we had gotten in the abundance. What amazed me most was that after I began looking for the benefits in the rejected appeal, I had a renewed peace in my spirit. God doesn't waste anything, even a rejected appeal.

God chose to show my husband, sixteen days after my fast, that the cautions I had were well-founded. We lost several thousands of dollars in the process. My husband now has a whole new outlook toward me.

I don't believe I would have survived the testing had I "only prayed." I am actually grateful for Him allowing this to have happened. God had planned so much more blessing through this testing. —A grateful wife

Evaluation for the Husband

1. Do you value your wife's counsel?

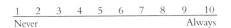

1	2	3	4	5	6	7	8	9	10
Never									Always

2. Have you received reproofs that could have been avoided by listening to the appeals of your wife?

1	2	3	4	5	6	7	8	9	10
Many									None

3. Do you feel that your wife's appeals are just a form of "sanctified nagging"?

1	2	3	4	5	6	7	8	9	10
Always									Never

4. Are you able to discern when God is speaking to you through your wife?

1	2	3	4	5	6	7	8	9	10
Never									Always

5. Do you react harshly to irritating attitudes in your wife when she makes an appeal?

1	2	3	4	5	6	7	8	9	10
Always									Never

6. Do you make your wife's appeals a matter of prayer before answering them?

1	2	3	4	5	6	7	8	9	10
Never									Always

7. When you reject an appeal, does your wife feel that you are rejecting her?

1	2	3	4	5	6	7	8	9	10
Always									Never

8. Are you in a position of not having higher authorities who can give you guidance and counsel?

1	2	3	4	5	6	7	8	9	10
Always									Never

O Lord, forgive me for not respecting each appeal from my wife and taking it before You in prayer, so that I can discern Your will in the matter. Forgive me for creating walls in my marriage because of not respecting the wisdom and value of the cautions that you give to my wife or that she has because of my weaknesses. Give me the grace to be a wise and kind husband.

Date prayed: _____   Initials _____

Evaluation for the Wife

1. **Does your husband know that you are ready to accept whatever decisions he makes?**

   1 2 3 4 5 6 7 8 9 10
   Never   Always

2. **Do you prepare your heart so that you are ready to thank God for the benefits that you will experience whether your appeal is accepted or rejected?**

   1 2 3 4 5 6 7 8 9 10
   Never   Always

3. **Have you demonstrated a content, grateful heart rather than a complaining spirit by thanking God when your appeal is rejected?**

   1 2 3 4 5 6 7 8 9 10
   Never   Always

4. **Have you learned to cry out to God along with the appeals that you make to your husband?**

   1 2 3 4 5 6 7 8 9 10
   Never   Always

5. **Does the heart of your husband safely trust in you because you have demonstrated past loyalty?**

   1 2 3 4 5 6 7 8 9 10
   Never   Always

6. **Do you accept your husband's decisions without a resistant spirit?**

   1 2 3 4 5 6 7 8 9 10
   Always   Never

7. **Is your idea of an appeal really just a form of "sanctified nagging" to get your way?**

   1 2 3 4 5 6 7 8 9 10
   Always   Never

8. **Have you committed the "sin of silence" by allowing a serious offense to continue and failing to go to a higher authority who can properly deal with your husband?**

   1 2 3 4 5 6 7 8 9 10
   Always   Never

O Lord, forgive me for focusing on my rejected appeal and believing that the only solution is to pray that You would somehow change my husband's heart about it. Forgive me for limiting You by not accepting his answer as something You can work through for my ultimate good.

Date prayed: _____   Initials _____

Chapter Seven

Deception Number Seven:

"Whatever is done in the marriage bed is permissible."

Why is this a deception?

This is one of the most serious and widespread of all the deceptions. It turns the holy state of matrimony into a "license" for unrestrained passions. It rules out the Holy Spirit's fruit of self-control and replaces it with self-indulgence. It turns genuine love into sensual lust and allows human passions to dictate the use of our bodies rather than the Holy Spirit Who dwells in them.

Marriage "counselors" who advocate this deception try to mask the degrading results by redefining God's parameters: "Within the context of marriage, virtually nothing is immoral, as long as both parties are comfortable with it and neither is harmed by it." This "guideline" is deceptive for the following reasons.

> *This deception simply reenacts the original temptation in which Adam and Eve decided for themselves what was right and what was wrong.*

1. It puts the couple in the place of God to decide for themselves what is right or wrong.

This approach to the marriage bed is an astonishing reenactment of the original temptation in the Garden of Eden. Essentially, Satan said to the first couple, "If you partake of the forbidden fruit, you shall be as gods, knowing good and evil." (See Genesis 3:5.) Marriage was instituted by God and must be regulated by His commandments rather than our sensual desires if we are to avoid the consequences so many are receiving in our day.

2. It presupposes that the body of each marriage partner belongs to himself or herself rather than to God.

God has the right of ownership to every person's body because He created it. Therefore, Scripture instructs us to "glorify God in your body, and in your spirit, which are God's" (I Corinthians 6:20). God created not only Adam and Eve, but every other person who is formed in the womb. The Lord said to Isaiah, "Thus saith the LORD, thy redeemer, and he that formed thee from the womb, I am the LORD that maketh all things" (Isaiah 44:24). Isaiah affirmed this fact by stating, "And now, saith the LORD that formed me from the womb to be his servant" (Isaiah 49:5).

God's ownership of us by creation is again declared to Jeremiah "Before I formed thee in the belly, I knew thee; and before thou camest forth out of the womb I sanctified thee, and I ordained thee a prophet unto the nations" (Jeremiah 1:5).

The Hebrew word translated *formed* is the very same word used by God to describe His creation of Adam: "And the LORD God formed man of the dust of the ground, and breathed into his nostrils the breath of life; and man became a living soul" (Genesis 2:7).

Since we do not own our own bodies, we have no right to decide for ourselves how to use them.

God has a rightful claim on our bodies not only because of creation but also because of redemption through the death of His Son Jesus. He paid the full price of Adam's transgression so that all who repent and receive the sacrifice of Christ are His by creation and redemption. "Forasmuch as ye know that ye were not redeemed with corruptible things, as silver and gold . . . But with the precious blood of Christ, as of a lamb without blemish and without spot" (I Peter 1:18–19).

3. It disregards God's warning to keep our bodies and souls pure and holy to avoid His judgment.

God gives firm warnings about serious consequences to all those who would defile their bodies, which are also the temples of the Holy Spirit. These warnings apply to both the married and the unmarried. "Know ye not that ye are the temple of God, and that the Spirit of God dwelleth in you? If any man defile the temple of God, him shall God destroy; for the temple of God is holy, which temple ye are. Let no man deceive himself" (I Corinthians 3:15–18). Anyone who believes that unrestrained passions are acceptable within marriage is allowing himself to be deceived and will suffer consequences.

God gave a list of moral prohibitions to the Ephesian believers. "But fornication, and all uncleanness, or covetousness, let it not be once named among you, as becometh saints; Neither filthiness, nor foolish talking, nor jesting, which are not convenient: but rather giving of thanks. For this ye know, that no whoremonger, nor unclean person, nor covetous man, who is an idolater, hath any inheritance in the kingdom of Christ and of God" (Ephesians 5:3–5).

Perverted activities advocated in the marriage bed violate one or more of the above restrictions. This makes the following warning very serious. "Let no man deceive you with vain words: for because of these things cometh the wrath of God upon the children of disobedience" (Ephesians 5:6).

4. It overlooks the deceptive nature of sin.

The stipulation that virtually anything is moral in marriage as long as both marriage partners are "comfortable" is completely unrealistic. It is void of any understanding of the nature of sin or of the nature of the human heart.

God has given every person a conscience to warn of evil. However, when we allow sin in our lives, the conscience is seared and soon

When we grieve the Holy Spirit, we become comfortable with sin and are unable to recognize it as wrong.

we are "comfortable" with that which at first we knew was wrong. It is all too easy for us to be "comfortable" with acts of sin because we live in an "adulterous and sinful generation." (See Mark 8:38.) The heart is described by God as "deceitful above all things, and desperately wicked" (Jeremiah 17:9). Therefore, Scripture warns us not to lean on our own understanding or trust in our own judgment. (See

Proverbs 3:5.) "He that trusteth in his own heart is a fool: but whoso walketh wisely, he shall be delivered" (Proverbs 28:26).

When we allow immoral acts in marriage, we grieve the Holy Spirit, Who abides in the temple of our bodies. The result is that His convicting power decreases and we no longer feel guilty about the impure act. Our "comfort" in doing it does not make it right. It may only confirm that we have quenched God's Spirit and have grown carnal and lukewarm toward the ways of God. Therefore, Scripture admonishes, "Exhort one another daily, while it is called To-day; lest any of you be hardened through the deceitfulness of sin" (Hebrews 3:13).

5. It turns genuine love into sensual lust.

Marriage was designed to be an expression of genuine love. However, that can be experienced only as both the husband and wife concentrate on a spirit of wholesome giving to each other. Lust turns giving into the selfish act of getting, and if it does not get what it wants, there is usually frustration and anger.

6. It gives license for activities that God categorically denounces and despises.

It is unthinkable that God would categorically condemn certain immoral activities for all believers and then excuse them for a person if he happened to participate in them with his wife. We are not referring here to the normal physical relationship between a husband and wife but to what Scripture refers to as uncleanness and inordinate affections. "Mortify therefore your members which are upon the earth; fornication, uncleanness, inordinate affection, evil concupiscence, and covetousness, which is idolatry" (Colossians 3:5).

> *It is unthinkable that God would condone in marriage what He condemns in the lives of all Christians.*

Such activities stir up the passions that are condemned in the first chapter of Romans. "Wherefore God also gave them up to uncleanness through the lusts of their own hearts, to dishonour their own bodies between themselves: Who changed the truth of God into a lie, and worshipped and served the creature more than the Creator, who is blessed for ever. Amen.

"For this cause God gave them up unto vile affections: for even their women did change the natural use into that which is against nature: And likewise also the men, leaving the natural use of the woman, burned in their lust one toward another; men with men working that which is unseemly, and receiving in themselves that recompence of their error which was meet [fitting]. And even as they did not like to retain God in their knowledge, God gave them over to a reprobate mind, to do those things which are not convenient" (Romans 1:24–28).

7. It overlooks the damage of "inordinate affections."

There is not only spiritual and psychological damage as a result of inordinate affections in marriage, but also physical and emotional consequences. When God designed the reproductive organs in a woman, He provided a triple protection against infection spreading to other parts of the body. There is no such protection in other organs. For example, the lack of protection in the mouth is readily confirmed by the fact that medication placed in the mouth quickly spreads throughout the body.

A married couple is not a law to themselves. They are members of the Body of Christ, so what they do affects every other believer.

8. It damages the Body of Christ.

The deceptive statement that virtually anything is permissible in the marriage bed fails to consider the fact that a married couple is not a law to themselves. If they are believers, they are both members of the Body of Christ, and therefore, whatever they do affects every other believer. This is the teaching of Scripture. "And whether one member suffer, all the members suffer with it" (I Corinthians 12:26).

God does not have different standards for the members of His Body. When one member violates His holy standards, he gives great occasion for the enemy to blaspheme the name of the Lord.

What couples allow, they will justify; what they will justify, they will condone; what they condone, they advocate. This is the tragedy of the Church in our day. Instead of being a "standard bearer" of God's light, our spiritual senses have been deadened and we are receiving worse consequences than the world around us. (One example of these consequences is the breakup of Christian families. The divorce rate among Christians is as high as that of unbelievers as a whole. Greater damage is done in a divorce situation among Christians when their children, and often the parents, go on in life disillusioned with the power of God's ways and truth.)

> *What parents permit in their marriage bed could be practiced by their children for generations to come.*

9. It fails to consider the damage that will be passed on to sons and daughters for generations to come.

When parents decide for themselves what is right or wrong in the marriage bed and develop unrestrained passions, they pass these lusts on to their children for several generations and to those whom their children will influence. Doing our own will is iniquity, even though it appears to be good and is accepted by others. Jesus did nothing of His own will, but only what His heavenly Father directed Him to do. (See John 5:30.)

Scripture warns that the iniquities of the fathers are passed on to their children to the third and fourth generations. "Visiting the iniquity of the fathers upon the children unto the third and fourth generation of them that hate me; And shewing mercy unto thousands of them that love me" (Exodus 20:5–6). What parents excuse between themselves, they will often judge as objectionable if done by their children. Yet, a willful child is the product of willful forefathers—all the way back to Adam.

10. It rejects the disciplines required for effective ministry.

Paul warned Timothy to flee youthful lusts and bring every appetite under the control of the Holy Spirit. He himself gave testimony that this was his personal program. "But I keep under my body, and bring it into subjection: lest that by any means, when I have preached to others, I myself should be a castaway" (I Corinthians 9:27). License in the marriage bed leads to loss of effective ministry.

What are the consequences of this deception?

When a husband expects or demands "inordinate affections" from his wife, her initial response is usually to feel defiled, unclean, and used. She will be quite aware that her husband is not demonstrating genuine love to her but is instead using her to satisfy the lusts of his own heart. The term *inordinate affections* is translated from the Greek word *pathos*, which means "suffering, i.e., pathos, a passion, lust." Men "suffer" from passionate desires and may put pressure on their wives to fulfill their lusts. A man given to lust is never satisfied but will be driven by those passions.

When lust is allowed or even encouraged in marriage, the love that God designed to bind the marriage together will be severely damaged. This not only damages the relationship between husband and wife, but also affects their children, who see the lack of genuine love between their parents. They will suffer from increased temptation and from the emotional damage of their parents' lack of love for each other.

Some of the tragic consequences of lust in the lives of husbands, their wives, and their children have been previously discussed. God also gives many additional reproofs designed to turn us back to Himself. Some of these pressures will be financial loss, loss of a wife's and children's respect, harsh or lenient discipline, frustration and anger, destruction of one's health, and spiritual defeat. There is also damage to the reputation of the Lord and the cause of Christ.

When lust is allowed to continue in a marriage relationship, it soon loses the pleasure that was once experienced by it. Therefore, the wages of lust is more lust, and soon a person is in the bondage of lustful addictions. "Hell and destruction are never full; so the eyes of man are never satisfied" (Proverbs 27:20). These lustful passions cannot be fulfilled by a wife and will soon seek fulfillment in adulterous relationships, either mental or physical.

> *When a husband arouses his sexual passions through lust and brings them to the marriage bed, he defiles the bed and degrades his wife.*

Why is this deception hard to overcome?

This deception is difficult to overcome, simply because of the confusion in the minds of men as to what lust is. The Lord went beyond the obvious and identified the root of lust when He declared, "Ye have heard that it was said by them of old time, Thou shalt not commit adultery: But I say unto you, That whosoever looketh on a woman to lust after her hath committed adultery with her already in his heart" (Matthew 5:27–28). Simply put, to admire or enjoy the beauty of a woman who is not your wife is lust that will defeat and destroy a man.

Those who promote this deception base it on one or two passages of Scripture which, when studied, do not support what these individuals are concluding. The first passage is Hebrews 13:4: "Marriage is honourable in all, and the bed undefiled: but whoremongers and adulterers God will judge."

Promoters of this deception usually quote only the first part of this verse, which gives the impression that everything in marriage is honorable and the bed cannot be defiled. Actually, the verse is saying just the opposite. The marriage that God designed is honorable for all people. Therefore, do not defile the marriage bed, because God will judge those who do. The second part of the verse identifies specific types of defilement that God will judge. The first type is a "whoremonger." The word *whoremonger* in Greek is *pornos*, which is the root of the word *porne,* from which we get the word *pornography.* The addiction to pornography is one of the greatest causes of defilement of the marriage bed. The dictionary defines *pornography* as "the presentation of explicit behavior, intended to arouse sexual excitement." The second type of defilement identified is adultery.

To be carnally minded is to be on the road to physical and spiritual death.

Other passages give further warnings about these sinful activities. "Knowing this, that the law is not made for a righteous man, but for the lawless and disobedient, for the ungodly and for sinners, for unholy and profane . . . for whoremongers, for them that defile themselves with mankind" (I Timothy 1:9–10).

Five times in the New Testament *pornos* is translated as *whoremonger(s)* and five times as *fornicator(s)*, as in the following verse. "Know ye not that the unrighteous shall not inherit the kingdom of God? Be not deceived: neither fornicators, nor idolaters, nor adulterers, nor effeminate, nor abusers of themselves with mankind"

(I Corinthians 6:9). The marriage bed can therefore be defiled by inordinate affections within the marriage or unfaithfulness outside of marriage.

Those who believe that there are no limitations to the marriage bed will also have to conclude that there is no need for self-control in this area because there is nothing to control. However, self-control is a fruit of the Spirit and is necessary at all times since we are in a constant battle between the flesh and the Spirit. "For the flesh lusteth against the Spirit, and the Spirit against the flesh: and these are contrary the one to the other: so that ye cannot do the things that ye would" (Galatians 5:17).

> *If lustful passions grieve the Holy Spirit, they will also grieve a Godly wife.*

In Galatians, God defines the activities that are to be rejected, whether in or out of the marriage. "Now the works of the flesh are manifest, which are these; Adultery, fornication, uncleanness, lasciviousness" (Galatians 5:19). Lasciviousness is a preoccupation with bodily and sexual pleasures apart from the direction and limits the Lord gives through His Word and His Spirit.

A second passage that is misused to justify the deception is in I Corinthians 6:12: "All things are lawful unto me." This part of the verse provides the desired license. However, the rest of the verse negates it. "But all things are not expedient: all things are lawful for me, but I will not be brought under the power of any."

Pornography is one of the strongest addictions there is. It conquers a man and makes him a slave of corrupt passions. The believers in the Corinthian church came out of a life of sensuality, and there was gross immorality in the church, for which Paul instructed discipline. Therefore, he repeats this in the same letter. "All things are lawful for me, but all things are not expedient: all things are lawful for me, but all things edify not. Let no man seek his own, but every man another's wealth" (I Corinthians 10:23–24). The instruction to "let no man seek his own" pleasures would directly contradict the false ideas in the deception pertaining to the marriage bed.

Moral freedom is not the right to do whatever we want. It is the power to do whatever God wants. Paul summarizes this point in

Galatians 5:13. "For, brethren, ye have been called unto liberty; only use not liberty for an occasion to the flesh, but by love serve one another." Rather than serving one another, the deception promotes the false idea of "using" one another for personal gratification.

What truths will overcome this deception?

The first step to conquer this deception is to repent of carnality and to become spiritually minded. When our souls make decisions based on the directives of the Spirit, we will be spiritually minded.

Denying the flesh on a daily basis is a practical way to conquer the passions of lust.

If, however, the soul makes decisions based on the impulses of the flesh, we will be carnally minded. This will produce moral slavery and many other consequences. "For to be carnally minded is death; but to be spiritually minded is life and peace. Because the carnal mind is enmity against God: for it is not subject to the law of God, neither indeed can be. So then they that are in the flesh cannot please God" (Romans 8:6-8).

When the conscience is violated with an act of moral impurity, the sensual drives are increased and the spiritual drives are diminished because the Holy Spirit is grieved. If men's immoral acts grieve the Holy Spirit, is it any wonder that these same acts also grieve a wife and make it difficult for her to respond to her husband? In order to overcome the pull of the flesh, we must walk in the Spirit. "This I say then, walk in the Spirit, and ye shall not fulfil the lusts of the flesh" (Galatians 5:16). It requires obedience to listen to the Spirit's promptings regarding what is right and what is wrong.

When a man bases his decisions on his physical senses and not on the Word of God, he will be "carnally minded." To escape this trap, a man must take careful heed to the instructions of God's Word. "Wherewithal shall a young man cleanse his way? by taking heed thereto according to thy word" (Psalm 119:9). It is for this reason that a man must engraft God's Word into his mind, will, and emotions and meditate on it day and night so he can obey it.

The next step is to overcome the appetites of the flesh by bringing the body into subjection. Paul stated, "I keep under my body and bring it into subjection" (I Corinthians 9:27). The phrase *keep under* literally means "to beat, disable, or subdue one's passions." *Subjection* means "to enslave." Therefore, the verse can be paraphrased, "I will disable my flesh and bring it into obedience to the Lordship of Christ!" To disable is to stop "feeding" the flesh, as the Lord directs. "Disable" the excuses your flesh gives for any form of disobedience, including sexual passions in marriage.

This is also the message of the following passages. "Mortify [put to death] therefore your members which are upon the earth; fornication, uncleanness, inordinate affection, evil concupiscence, and covetousness, which is idolatry" (Colossians 3:5). We must "put off concerning the former conversation [lifestyle] the old man, which is corrupt according to the deceitful lusts; And be renewed in the spirit of your mind; And that you put on the new man, which after God is created in righteousness and true holiness" (Ephesians 4:22–24).

Confirming Testimonies

How a Daily Denial
Conquered a Deadly Deception

Ever since I was young, my family focused on the outward appearance of people, especially what women wore. Was she dumpy, plain, or good-looking? With this emphasis on externals, I thought nothing of looking at other women, until I was married. My wife took offense at my "looks." This brought insecurity to her (about how she looked and a self-consciousness). We came to Christ at a Basic Seminar shortly after we were married. I learned that my "old man" was put to death with Christ and that I was "a new creature in Christ." Yet somehow I was not experiencing this truth in anything but my head.

I was very selfish in the marriage bed. I never considered anything but my needs. I made her feel like something was wrong with her. I thought my appetite was totally "normal." I see now that my view of marriage was really just "license" to allow my lusts to run unchecked. My wife felt doubtful that she was able to please or satisfy me, and she desperately needed the assurance of my love for her. What I didn't realize was that my lust was severely damaging any hopes for her to have that need met from me.

The problem was that I was so used to enjoying lust that I couldn't imagine living without it, yet I saw its damaging effects on my wife. I tried throwing the "hot potato" in her lap and making it her fault. I'm glad for her pursuit of holiness in the marriage bed. She wouldn't accept the guilt I was trying to put on her. There were times, in the marriage bed, that I considered her, and it was amazing how she responded to genuine love. There was a fulfillment! On the contrary, when I was mechanical and selfishly pursued her to fulfill my own desires, her spirit seemed to leave her, like something died. She knew she was not cherished.

I finally came to the place where I realized that I was helpless, power-less, and completely unable to help myself. I had caused my wife so much pain and I knew it, yet I was so self-centered that it really didn't seem to truly bother me. I was unable to experience a genuine brokenness over my sin. "The sacrifices of God are a broken spirit: a broken and contrite heart, O God, thou wilt not despise" (Psalm 51:17). In desperation and at the end of my rope, I cried out to God. It seemed so helpless an effort, yet it was all I had. If God did not do something, I would surely be unable to change, and all hope for a loving marriage would be lost. "Create in me a clean heart, O God; and renew a right spirit within me" (Psalm 51:10).

What God first showed me was that my lust was really rebellion and disobedience. I began to realize that my flesh was very strong and in control and that "declaring war" against the flesh would be difficult. The first "battle strategy" the Lord gave me was to purpose to daily deny my flesh something, as He directed. This initially meant food, since food was also such a controlling part of my life. Daily I allowed the Lord to decide what it would be: a second helping, a candy bar, dessert, etc., or sometimes even a meal. "The flesh wars against the Spirit and the Spirit against the flesh." It was amazing how much this simple exercise enabled me to hear the Spirit's promptings and disable the flesh's pulls. Each day I asked the Holy Spirit what He wanted me to deny in my life. At the end of the day, I wrote down in my daily planner whether or not I denied it.

For the first time in my life I saw what a pull the flesh really had upon me. God used this process to strengthen His Spirit in me. When His Spirit was stronger, the flesh lost its pull on me. I felt free of it. I began to *really enjoy food for the first time in my life! I was no longer its slave. At the same time, I was becoming more aware of, and able to identify, lust in the marriage. As I became more sensitive to the Spirit's promptings about what I ate, I also became aware of His promptings in those special times with my wife. I began asking her for forgiveness each time I put myself ahead of her.*

It wasn't easy for my wife, but she didn't stop forgiving me. She was such a big help! We spent a lot of late nights up, but it was worth it every time. The enemy's work in our life and marriage is being thwarted and God's Spirit is being strengthened. I found that the flesh is truly no friend, although it promises so much. I see now that this in fact is a battle that must be fought to win. I also realized that I will either win or lose based on my obedience to the Spirit. "The flesh wars against the Spirit and the Spirit against the flesh." I found that this verse is very true, but it is also true that "greater is He that is in us than he that is in the world."

—An unshackled husband

How a Simple Prayer Protected a Marriage Bed

Thank you for addressing this delicate issue in the spirit in which you did. A burden has been lifted! The guilt and pressure that "anything goes" in the marriage bed was confusing to me. I would try to accept this thinking in my mind, but my spirit never had a peace. What confused me even more was that churches were encouraging women to "play the part" in order to keep their husbands. Whatever happened to love and respect for one another keeping a couple together?

Since lust had played such a major part in our marriage bed, we really didn't know what to do. We both agreed that what you were saying was right, but how do you break the routine and begin anew? So I came up to you, Connie, and simply asked, "What do I wear? How do we act?"

Thank you for suggesting we pray for God's protection before coming together. I am writing to testify that it works. My husband prayed, "Lord, please protect this marriage bed from lust. Let us experience genuine love for one another Your way." We fervently prayed this, sick of our routine and desiring something deeper. God heard our heart-cry and barred lust from our bedroom. It was so fulfilling for both of us!

There were times that we forgot to pray and lust would sneak back in. I immediately asked my husband, "Could you pray? I feel like it's coming back." He would pray right there and then and a peace and sweetness returned. Thank you for sharing your lives with us! God bless you.

—*An amazed wife*

How the Snare of Pride Led a Man Into the Destructiveness of Lust

Satan's snare is pride! As soon as he gets us to believe that we are capable of deciding for ourselves what is right and what is wrong, we are drawn into that snare. It is there he will take us down.

I am so grateful for your taking the time to talk with me. I am writing to thank you and explain what really benefited me in our conversation together.

As you know we have been married for over 25 years. All throughout our marriage I have been receiving the consequences of lust without realizing it (humiliation, lack of respect, financial loss, broken relationships with my wife and children, and even disease).

I sincerely believed I did not have a lust problem. I appreciate how you simplified what lust is by simply asking me, "Do you look at other women to admire their beauty?" I am embarrassed to say this, but I remember thinking that I did not have a problem like you did. I now realize that mine was worse! I was not even fighting it. Your struggle was in the small circle of your dreams; your awake life was under control; mine was in my conscious thought. My conscience was not even working. I had deadened it by failing to respond to it. I had failed to agree with the Lord's definition of lust, "If a man looks upon a woman to lust after her in his heart, he has committed adultery in his mind."

My wife is a very submissive and Godly woman. She knew something was wrong. Our intimate times together were characterized by a deep sadness on my wife's part. I built up walls that I hid behind. I was a "quiet" man who spent much time alone after work. I made excuses for myself, saying I needed to do other things. I effectively closed my wife out of my private life by always being too busy or too tired, etc. Ironically, I justified what I was doing by telling myself that my wife was not able to fulfill my needs, especially my emotional ones. I blamed her so that I did not have to deal with my problem of being unfaithful to her and enjoying the beauty of other women. Amazingly,

I really believed that she was the problem. Secretly, I suppose, I was even hoping that she too was unfaithful so I would not look so bad.

I came to find out that pride was at the root of my lust. I decided to do whatever I wanted to do if I felt I had a good reason for it, or could justify it in some other way (which I found many ways of doing). When you shared the truth of Romans 2:1, I saw the incredible accuracy of it. I was judging others of exactly what I was doing . . . especially my wife! It was not that she did not want to talk and have a relationship with me; I just pushed her away so I could continue on in my error. Pride is so blinding! Thank you for opening my eyes and seeing my sin as God does. Had you not have done it I would still be blaming my wife for what in acuality I was doing. I thank God for the accuracy of His word and for your pointing me to it. I am very grateful to the Spirit of God for opening my eyes to what would have surely destroyed my marriage if not my life.

—A repentant husband

Evaluation for the Husband

1. Have you believed the deception that "anything goes" in the marriage bed?

   1 2 3 4 5 6 7 8 9 10
   Always   Never

2. Have you related financial reproofs, such as debt, to a lack of self-control in your life?

   1 2 3 4 5 6 7 8 9 10
   Never   Always

3. Would your wife say that you put your physical desires ahead of her?

   1 2 3 4 5 6 7 8 9 10
   Always   Never

4. Do you have a struggle in overcoming lust and anger?

   1 2 3 4 5 6 7 8 9 10
   Always   Never

5. Do you believe that fulfillment in marriage comes more by spiritual oneness than physical pleasures?

   1 2 3 4 5 6 7 8 9 10
   Always   Never

6. Are you denying yourself something each day, as the Lord directs?

   1 2 3 4 5 6 7 8 9 10
   Always   Never

7. Have you justified sensuality based on marriage books that promote it?

   1 2 3 4 5 6 7 8 9 10
   Always   Never

8. Do you ask God to protect your marriage bed from lust?

   1 2 3 4 5 6 7 8 9 10
   Never   Always

---

*O **Lord**,* forgive me for believing the deception that taking what I want will bring fulfillment apart from Your limitations. I do acknowledge that I have allowed my flesh to be in control. I confess this thinking as wrong and desire to be an obedient son by listening to Your Spirit's promptings. I will listen to You daily as You speak to me through Your Word. I will deny myself something daily, as You direct, to feed Your Spirit within me and disable my flesh.

Date prayed: _____   Initials _____

Evaluation for the Wife

1. **Have you believed the deception that "anything goes" in the marriage bed?**

   1   2   3   4   5   6   7   8   9   10
   Always   Never

2. **Have you felt inadequate to meet your husband's physical needs without becoming seductive?**

   1   2   3   4   5   6   7   8   9   10
   Never   Always

3. **Have you justified sensuality based on marriage books that promote it?**

   1   2   3   4   5   6   7   8   9   10
   Always   Never

4. **Do you believe that fulfillment in marriage comes more by physical pleasures than spiritual oneness?**

   1   2   3   4   5   6   7   8   9   10
   Never   Always

5. **Are you willing to help your husband in daily victory by being his accountability partner?**

   1   2   3   4   5   6   7   8   9   10
   Never   Always

6. **Have you released your husband from the hurts of his moral failures?**

   1   2   3   4   5   6   7   8   9   10
   Never   Always

7. **Are you willing to deny your flesh daily to strengthen your spirit?**

   1   2   3   4   5   6   7   8   9   10
   Never   Always

8. **Do you realize how lust affects your habits in overspending, overeating, and overreacting?**

   1   2   3   4   5   6   7   8   9   10
   Never   Always

> **O Lord**, forgive me for believing the deception that taking what I want will bring fulfillment apart from Your limitations. I do acknowledge that I have allowed my flesh to be in control. I confess this thinking as wrong and desire to be an obedient daughter by listening to Your Spirit's promptings. I will listen to You daily as You speak to me through Your Word. I will deny myself something daily, as You direct, to feed Your Spirit within me and disable my flesh.
>
> Date prayed: _____   Initials _____